George Kennan for Our Time

People for Our Time

A collection of books from Northern Illinois University Press

A list of titles in this collection is available at cornellpress.cornell.edu.

George Kennan for Our Time

Lee Congdon

Northern Illinois University Press
An imprint of Cornell University Press

Ithaca and London

First published 2022 by Cornell University Press

Printed in the United States of America

Library of Congress Cataloging-in-Publication Data

Names: Congdon, Lee, 1939– author.
Title: George Kennan for our time / Lee Congdon.
Description: Ithaca [New York] : Northern Illinois University Press, an imprint of Cornell University Press, 2022. | Series: People for our time | Includes bibliographical references and index.
Identifiers: LCCN 2021053394 | ISBN 9781501765186 (paperback) | ISBN 9781501765193 (pdf) | ISBN 9781501765209 (epub)
Subjects: LCSH: Kennan, George F. (George Frost), 1904–2005. | Ambassadors—United States—Biography. | Historians—United States—Biography. | United States—Foreign relations—Philosophy. | United States—Foreign relations—20th century. | United States—Politics and government—20th century—Philosophy.
Classification: LCC E748.K374 C665 2022 | DDC 327.2092 [B]—dc23/eng/20211106
LC record available at https://lccn.loc.gov/2021053394

To Carol

Contents

George Kennan for Our Time

Introduction

ON THE EDGE OF THE ABYSS

Ours is a time of mounting crises, international and national. Since the tenure of Henry Kissinger, a practitioner of Realpolitik, those charged with the conduct of America's foreign policy have set aside consideration of the national interest in favor of crusades to remake the world in America's image, by force if necessary. The result has been protracted wars in Iraq and Afghanistan and insistent calls for military confrontations with Syria and Iran. Having persuaded themselves that America is "the indispensable nation," as former secretary of state Madeleine Albright said, diplomatic officials have refused to adopt balance-of-power policies when dealing with other great powers—those in possession of nuclear weapons. When the Soviet Union collapsed, the United States stood as the lone superpower—but not for long. Despite some ongoing problems, Russia recovered from seventy-four years of communist misrule and China emerged as a credible rival for world leadership. Rather than view these new realities as incentives to conduct genuine diplomacy (the adjustment of competing interests), successive administrations have chosen to act internationally with an air of superiority.

It is past time to consider anew the warnings and counsels of the late George Kennan, twentieth-century America's most distinguished diplomat. Kennan served as ambassador to the Soviet Union and Yugoslavia and as a senior official in Switzerland, Germany, Czechoslovakia, and the Baltic states. He was for a time the deputy commandant for foreign affairs at the National War College and the director of the Policy Planning Staff at the Department of State. He played a key role in the development of the Marshall Plan that fueled postwar Europe's recovery and he formulated the containment policy that governed US actions and reactions during the Cold War. From 1933, when he first went to Moscow, to 1953, when he retired from the Foreign Service, he was involved in virtually every one of the nation's major foreign policy decisions.

In the course of that involvement, Kennan drafted countless papers, two of which achieved historic status: the "Long Telegram" transmitted to the State Department from Moscow in 1946 and "The Sources of Soviet Conduct," published in *Foreign Affairs* in 1947. Always he sought not only to offer his judgments but to polish his prose, because he was a writer as well as a diplomat. After leaving the Foreign Service, he joined Princeton's Institute for Advanced Study, where he embarked on a career as a historian with a literary bent.

For the remainder of his long life (he died at age 101), Kennan was a permanent member of the institute and the author of highly regarded histories, primarily concerning US-Soviet relations and the diplomatic origins of the Great War. He was not, however, interested in the past for its own sake but for the lessons that it imparted to the present. That explains why he continued to lecture and write on contemporary foreign policy, often regarding relations with the Soviet Union but just as often regarding matters of more general concern. Congress regularly invited him to testify, but although its members treated him with respect they were reluctant to adopt his policy recommendations. Despite the fact that, unlike so many of his generation, he never entertained the least sympathy for the Bolshevik Revolution and during World War II was even considered to be too anticommunist, he had come to be regarded as a Cold War dove, soft on communism.

Nothing could have been further from the truth. The destruction of lives and material culture resulting from the war against Germany and Japan, combined with the development of nuclear weapons, convinced Kennan that the principal responsibility of diplomats must be to prevent an apocalyptic war. He made every effort to convince US and Western foreign policy establishments that the choice before them was not between war and submission, and that it was possible to conduct meaningful negotiations with the Soviet Union without glossing over conflicting interests. A patient policy of containment—political, not military—would preserve the peace. Kennan always believed that the Soviet Union would eventually collapse under its own weight, and in the end he proved to be right.

The threat of nuclear war was not Kennan's only preoccupation. He argued against a foreign policy that aimed to democratize the world. A realist in foreign policy, he maintained that the United States should act in the world only in defense of the national interest, narrowly defined. Those, he insisted, who agitated for a morally driven policy failed to recognize that government is an agent, not a principal. Its primary obligation is to the interests of the national society it represents, not to the moral enthusiasms of members of that society. What was needed, therefore, was a policy distinguished above all by its restraint. That was particularly important when dealing with nuclear powers such as Russia and China, which had legitimate interests of their own. He saw no reason why the United States should take it on itself to offer unsolicited political instruction to the governments of those historic lands.

Other than the great powers, Kennan believed that there were only a few world areas of strategic importance to the United States—principally Europe and Japan. He never thought his country had important security interests in the lands of the Near East, and he therefore advocated a complete withdrawal from that troubled part of the world. In opposition to almost every member of the foreign policy establishment, he identified himself as an isolationist, the prevailing posture in America until early in the twentieth century.

The primary business of the United States, in Kennan's judgment, should be to put its own house in order. He judged America's national crises to be even more threatening than those it faced internationally. Among the former he counted the vulnerabilities of mass democracy, the dangers of uncontrolled immigration, the despoilment of nature, the growing number of addictions, the unmistakable signs of decadence, and, above all, the spiritual emptiness. Where Judeo-Christian moral law was once universally honored, even if more in the breach than in the observance, it had come under sustained attack. The country had lost its moral compass along with any agreed upon principles of government.

Although Kennan was well aware that his views concerning international and national life went against the American grain, he never tired of efforts to alert his countrymen to the fateful road on which they were traveling. In this account, I have tied him closely to his writings, because texts do not exhaust their own meanings. A web of personal and historical events always give them wider and deeper significance. It matters that Kennan was born before World War I and judged America to have been a better country then than it became after World War II. It matters, too, that he was a committed, if unorthodox, Christian who viewed the world through tragic lenses. The lessons for our time that I discuss here bear the indelible marks of a remarkable life and a turbulent era in the history of the United States and of the world.

Following a brief biographical chapter, chapter 2 traces the history of American foreign policy from the realism and restraint of George Washington and Alexander Hamilton to the moralizing interventionism of Woodrow Wilson and his successors. It places Kennan squarely in the realist camp and identifies the principles that informed his teachings and guided his conduct during long years in the Foreign Service. Chapters 3 and 4 discuss Kennan's application of his principles to relations with Russia, Eastern Europe, and the countries of the Far and Near East. Chapter 5 offers an account of the foreign policy establishment's rejection of almost all of Kennan's advice from the Vietnam War on and of that rejection's often disastrous results. Chapter 6 turns to Kennan's critique of an American society he believed to be headed for the abyss, and chapter 7 presents his hopes for its revivification. Chapter 8 explains Kennan's call for a return to representative government and concludes with a plea to his countrymen not to succumb to despair.

1

A Brief Biography

In his memoirs, George Frost Kennan confessed that he was not the cool, detached diplomat many took him to be, that his public self was a persona, a role he assumed in an effort to shield a shy, introverted nature and to meet the demands of his profession. Born in Milwaukee on February 16, 1904, Kennan never knew his mother, Florence James Kennan, who died of peritonitis shortly after giving him birth. His tax-lawyer father, Kossuth Kent Kennan, descended from a Scottish family (the surname being originally McKennan) that arrived in the United States from Northern Ireland early in the eighteenth century; he was named after Lajos Kossuth, the liberal leader of Hungary's abortive 1848–49 revolution and war of independence against Austria.

Kennan took great pride in his family. "The family as I knew it," he told a close friend, the Hungarian American historian John Lukacs, "still bore strongly the markings of an eighteenth-century experience and discipline." He was equally proud of the fact that his family's tradition of farming bred into it a love of the rural life, a strong work ethic, and a spirit of independence. Another George Kennan, a cousin of Kennan's grandfather, lent a modicum of fame to the family as a result of his investigation of the tsarist government's Siberian exile system.

The Social Revolutionaries with whom Kennan's relative came into contact in Siberia were relatively moderate Populists (for whom the peasantry, not the proletariat, was the revolutionary class). They were not, he insisted in *Siberia and the Exile System* (1891), crazy fanatics, but civilized and intelligent men and women. In view of the cruel and barbarous conditions to which they were subjected, their resort to terrorism seemed to him not only unsurprising but perfectly reasonable. He did not defend their crimes, but he could understand how they might turn to violence when they were subjected to intolerable outrages and indignities and had no peaceful or legal means of redress.

In his introduction to a reprint of *Siberia and the Exile System*, George Kennan painted a respectful portrait of his relative, but he did not think that he had taken full account of the indiscriminate campaign of terrorism that some of the revolutionaries had waged against the government, or of the extent to which their criminal actions had provoked a response that fell on them and others less guilty. He had come to think, in fact, that the tsarist government's treatment of revolutionaries had been, if anything, lenient: "It is after all a habit of political regimes to resist their own violent overthrow." What is more, as Kennan told the Hungarian-born interviewer George Urban, his namesake's assumption was that "if one could only overthrow the old Czarist autocracy, something much better would follow." He added: "Have we learned anything from this lesson?"

That having been said, Kennan emphasized that his forebear enjoyed a position of respectability in all sections of American opinion, but particularly among the members of the educated, well-bred, old-American upper class. Such renown, coupled with a common name and date of birth, helped to create in Kennan an almost mystical bond with his distant relative, though he would have been unaware of the letter the latter had addressed to his father in 1912: "You have a son who bears my name. It would be a great satisfaction to me if I could feel that certain things which have personal or historical interest and which have been closely associated with my work could be transferred to him when he becomes old enough to understand them and take an interest in them."

The elder George Kennan would not, had he lived longer, have been disappointed. The subject of this study explained why in his memoirs:

> Both of us devoted large portions of our adult life to Russia and her problems. We were both expelled from Russia by the Russian government of our day, at comparable periods of our careers. Both of us founded organizations to assist refugees from Russian despotism. Both wrote and lectured profusely. Both played the guitar. Both owned and loved particular sailboats of similar construction. Both eventually became members of the National Institute of Arts and Letters. Both had occasion to plead at one time or another for greater understanding in America for Japan and her geopolitical problems vis-à-vis the Asian mainland.

In 1912, Kennan's father took his family to Kassel, Germany, and young George achieved fluency in the German language by the end of the six-month sojourn. To be sure, he had taken classes in German at Milwaukee State Normal, the grade school he attended before being sent, in 1917, to St. John's Military Academy, a high-church Episcopalian institution in Delafield, Wisconsin. He credited the latter institution with having contributed to the formation of his character. It was there, he recalled later in life, that he learned to dress neatly and to keep his room in order.

In the fall of 1921, Kennan entered Princeton University, primarily because, as a senior at St. John's, he had read and been moved by F. Scott Fitzgerald's *This Side of Paradise.* Like Fitzgerald himself, the novel's protagonist, Amory Blaine, attends Princeton; like Kennan, he is from Wisconsin and is, as Fitzgerald put it, "unbearably lonely, desperately unhappy." Kennan found himself confronted with the greater sophistication and smoother manners of many of his fellow students. He came to know few of them and was known by fewer. History was his declared major, but his memories of the program of studies were dismal; with one exception he was little influenced by his instructors. That exception, however, was a notable one—Raymond Sontag, a distinguished historian of European diplomacy. "The impression of his approach to [his] subject," Kennan recalled, "skeptical, questioning, disillusioned without being discouraged, was indelible."

Sontag was clearly instrumental in leading Kennan, on graduation, to try for the newly organized Foreign Service. To that end, he engaged a tutor to help him prepare for the exams, which he then passed. Thus began, in the fall of 1926, a storied and often controversial career. Toward the end of summer 1927, Kennan received assignment to his first permanent post, at Hamburg. He came to love that city, he wrote in the diaries he had begun to keep at age eleven, as he had loved no other.

That helps to explain why he was so sickened when he visited the German city after World War II. From July 24 to August 3, 1943, the Allies had subjected it to a series of devastating air raids—codenamed Operation Gomorrah. On one night, July 27–28, Allied planes unloaded nine thousand tons of high explosives and incendiary bombs that created an unimaginable firestorm; thirty thousand men, women, and children perished as a result of the attack. "For the first time," Kennan wrote in his diaries, "I felt an unshakable conviction that no momentary military advantage . . . could have justified this stupendous, careless destruction of civilian life and material values, built up laboriously by human hands over the course of centuries for purposes having nothing to do with this war."

Although Kennan enjoyed his time in interwar Hamburg, he became acutely aware of the limits of his education and resolved to resign from the Foreign Service in order to pursue graduate studies. His path in life would have taken an irreversible turn had he not been informed at the last minute that he could receive training as a specialist in a language little known within the service— Chinese, Japanese, Arabic, or Russian.

Kennan chose Russian, in part because of what he believed to be its future career promise but also because of his relative's example. Before he could begin his formal studies, however, he had to serve twelve to eighteen months in the Russian field, which, because the United States did not then maintain relations with the USSR, meant the Baltic states, only recently freed from Russian rule. In the summer of 1929, after several months in Tallinn, Estonia (his favorite), and Riga, Latvia, Kennan moved on to Berlin, where for a year he studied Russian subjects at the Friedrich-Wilhelms-Universität's Seminary for Oriental Languages. The following year he moved to the university proper, where he enrolled in courses in Russian history taught by two distinguished professors: Otto Hoetsch and Karl Stählin.

This was the time of Christopher Isherwood's *Berlin Stories*, the years of the Depression and the rise of Adolf Hitler, but Kennan's world was not that of "Mr. Ishevoo" and Sally Bowles. He kept largely to himself, although he did meet Annelise Sørensen, whom he married in Kristiansand, Norway, her hometown, on September 11, 1931. After a honeymoon in Vienna, the couple headed for Riga, where Kennan took up a new post in the Russian section of the American legation, one that he manned until autumn 1933. On November 16 of that year President Franklin Roosevelt, his eyes fixed on Nazi Germany and militaristic Japan, recognized the Soviet government and named William C. Bullitt as the US ambassador.

Kennan had serious reservations concerning the wisdom of the president's decision (perhaps because the first George Kennan had opposed recognition), but having prepared himself for service in Russia he was pleased when Bullitt asked him to serve as an interpreter and aide. Unlike the skeptical Kennan, Bullitt arrived in Joseph Stalin's Russia with high expectations, confident that he could overcome communist suspicion and hostility; he left within three years, disillusioned and embittered.

Bullitt's successor was Joseph E. Davies, one of those who fit Vladimir Lenin's description of a "useful idiot." An investment banker married to General Foods heiress Marjorie Merriweather Post, Davies persuaded himself that the Moscow Trials of the late 1930s were fully justified by the threat that the accused posed to the government. In *Mission to Moscow*, Davies wrote that "the state had established its case, at least to the extent of proving the existence of a widespread conspiracy and plot among the political leaders against the Soviet government."

Not in Kennan's view. As Davies's interpreter, he attended the Second Moscow Trial (January 23–30, 1937)—of the so-called Anti-Soviet Trotskyite Center. In the dock were seventeen men, most notably Yuri Pyatakov, an economic administrator who had played a pivotal role in the industrialization of the USSR but who had sided with Leon Trotsky in the struggle to succeed Lenin; and Karl Radek, a Bolshevik intellectual well known in the West. According to the indictment, members of the alleged center planned to sabotage industry, restore capitalism, spy for the Germans and Japanese, and assassinate Soviet leaders.

These were, as Kennan recognized, fantastic charges, but Stalin could not, he reasoned, allow his victims to disappear from public view with an aura of martyrdom about their heads; they had to be publicly humiliated. They knew that they would be shot but still played their roles, some out of consideration for their families but some, according to Kennan, for another reason: "[Sergei] Mrach-kovski and [Nikolai] Muralov because they were sincere fanatical old Bolsheviks and had been convinced by their jailors that they owed it to the Revolution to do this"—precisely the argument that Arthur Koestler advanced in *Darkness at Noon*, his famous novel of the trials.

Unhappy to be subject to the authority of a man of Davies's stamp, Kennan was relieved when, in mid-1937, Washington summoned him home to take over the Russian desk in the State Department's Division of European Affairs. He served in that capacity for a year before being assigned to Prague, where he arrived on September 29, 1938, the day that the Munich Conference opened. In Hitler's "Brown House" residence, Britain and France agreed that Czechoslovakia should cede to Germany those areas with a predominantly German-speaking population that rimmed the historic provinces of Bohemia and Moravia. However shocking this was to many observers, Kennan believed that the peacemakers after World War I had made a serious mistake when they left three million Germans in what he saw as a hopelessly artificial successor to the Austro-Hungarian monarchy.

Kennan stayed on in Prague as an officer charged with maintaining custody of US diplomatic files and preserving US property. When, however, Hitler launched World War II in Europe by invading Poland on September 1, 1939, the State Department transferred him to Berlin. There he remained until, four days after the

Japanese attacked Pearl Harbor, Hitler declared war on the United States and ordered the Gestapo to take American embassy personnel, Kennan included, into custody. On December 14, 1941, he and 113 other Americans were herded onto a train bound for Bad Nauheim, a spa north of Frankfurt.

For the next five months, the Germans, under the command of an SS officer, held the Americans incommunicado in Jeschke's Grand Hotel, which had been closed since the outbreak of war. With reluctance, Kennan assumed responsibility for the discipline he knew would be required to make the best of the situation; it was a thankless task that did little to improve his jaundiced view of human nature. In order to maintain morale, he and others organized the "Badheim University," under whose auspices he offered a class on Russian history, thus launching an illustrious, if intermittent, teaching career. The study of history, he told his receptive students, offered the surest guide to the formation of public policy. He could take the class no further than the reign of Alexander I (1801–25) because in May 1942 he and the others learned that they were to be exchanged for German internees in the United States. After release they boarded a train that carried them to Lisbon, where they took passage to the United States aboard a Swedish ship.

In July 1944, after assignments in Portugal and London, Kennan returned to the Soviet Union at the request of Ambassador Averell Harriman. In an October letter to his sister Jeanette he expressed his indescribable satisfaction at being back again in the midst of a people with such pulsating warmth and vitality. He did not have the same feelings for the Soviet regime, much less for Stalin, of whom he later offered the following description: "This was a man of incredible criminality, of a criminality effectively without limits; a man apparently foreign to the very experience of love; without pity or mercy."

When the war in Europe ended in May 1945, Kennan could not be counted among those for whom euphoria was the dominant emotion, because he viewed with alarm the expansion of Soviet power into Eastern Europe, a condition that, for the foreseeable future, seemed to him to be irreversible. That was not a view shared by those in Washington who believed that wartime collaboration between the two countries would continue into the postwar period. Among them was President Harry Truman, who, in a Navy Day speech on October 27, 1945, appealed for Soviet-American cooperation. Invoking his country's traditional equation of private with public morality, he promised not to relent in his effort to bring the golden rule into the international affairs of the world.

With the war over and his power again secure, Stalin returned the Soviet Union to the prewar atmosphere of terror and Kennan wanted, almost desperately, to return to the United States. An opportunity presented itself only when, on February 22, 1946, he transmitted to the State Department the now famous "Long Telegram" (just over five thousand words in length), prompted by a request for help in understanding Stalin's refusal to join the World Bank and the International Monetary Fund.

With Ambassador Harriman's encouragement, Kennan set to work. In one section of the telegram, he argued that the Kremlin's paranoid view of the world was rooted in Russia's traditional sense of insecurity, made worse by Marxism's insistence on the inevitability and necessity of conflict. Here he touched on an important question: whether Soviet policy was dictated by Marxist dogma or Russian nationalism. His answer was that the two went hand in hand—the Soviet leaders did pursue expansionist goals similar to those of the tsars, but Marxism was also important, even if Stalin was less of a true believer than Lenin. That is why the Soviets operated on two planes: official and subterranean. On the one they observed diplomatic formalities and participated in international organizations such as the United Nations; on the other they worked underground to subvert the West while denying any responsibility.

Despite its challenges, Kennan concluded that relations with the USSR could be maintained, as long as realism governed policy. Stalin and other Soviet leaders were opportunists who would not assume unnecessary risks. They would withdraw when met with strong resistance, by which Kennan did not mean military engagement; rational, unemotional political firmness would do the trick.

The effect produced in Washington by the Long Telegram was, as Kennan later observed, nothing short of sensational. "Suddenly," he wrote in his memoirs, "my official loneliness came in fact to an end—at least for a period of two to three years. My reputation was made. My voice now carried." And so it did. Two months after he sent the telegram, he received appointment as the deputy commandant for foreign affairs at the newly established National War College in Washington, DC. He was to be responsible for the political side of the military-political curriculum.

Among the papers Kennan prepared in the winter of 1946–47 was one written at the request of Secretary of the Navy James Forrestal. Entitled "The Sources of Soviet Conduct" and published in *Foreign Affairs*, the article constituted a literary version of the Long Telegram. Speaking unofficially, Kennan signed the article with an X, but his identity did not long remain a secret. Once outed he became known as the architect of the postwar policy of containment of the Soviet Union, which, to his dismay, most people understood to refer to a military, rather than a political, strategy. Worse, it took the form of a doctrine to be applied universally, rather than a principle adjusted to meet particular situations. Before the article appeared and controversy erupted, however, Secretary of State George C. Marshall informed Kennan that he would have to leave the War College in order to become the director of State's new Policy Planning Staff (PPS), charged with identifying America's long-term foreign policy objectives.

The PPS was formally established on May 5, 1947, and on May 23 Kennan forwarded to Under Secretary of State Dean Acheson its first recommendation—to provide economic aid to Western Europe. The staff believed that such aid should be directed not to combating communism as such but to restoring the economic health of Europe. In the speech on the Marshall Plan that he delivered at Harvard University on June 5, 1947, Secretary Marshall signaled total acceptance of the PPS recommendation; it was, Kennan said years later, a great act of statesmanship. "Diplomacy was not his professional element," he wrote in praise of Marshall in a 1959 letter to the *New York Times.* But he was "an American gentleman at his best—honorable, courteous, devoid of arrogance, exacting of others but even more of himself, intolerant only of cowardice, deviousness, and cynicism."

In the same recommendation to Acheson, Kennan added a subsection calling for a public clarification of the doctrine announced by President Truman before a joint session of Congress on March 12, 1947. In approving aid to Greece and Turkey to confront the threat of communism, the president had said: "I believe that it must be the policy of the United States to support free peoples who are resisting attempted subjugation by armed minorities or by outside pressures." Kennan thought it better to speak of principles than of doctrines. It should be made clear, he wrote, almost in desperation, that the doctrine did not constitute a blank check to give economic and military aid to any area in the world where the communists showed signs of being successful. Aid to Greece and Turkey should be regarded as a particular remedy for a particular problem.

Unfortunately, the government ignored Kennan's recommendation as well as his opposition to the establishment of the United Nations (which he believed could not, as an international organization for the preservation of peace and security, take the place of a well-conceived and realistic foreign policy), the creation of Israel (which he believed would generate a problem for which there could be no peaceful solution), and the organization of NATO (which he felt reflected too great a preoccupation with military rivalry). For these reasons and because of a general feeling of frustration, he decided to step down as director of the PPS and, in June 1950, to take a leave of absence from government service. At the invitation of Director J. Robert Oppenheimer, the wartime head of the Los Alamos Laboratory, he moved to Princeton to pursue historical studies at the Institute for Advanced Study (IAS).

But Kennan's public service was not yet ended. President Truman appointed him to succeed retiring admiral Alan Kirk as US ambassador to the Soviet Union; he accepted the appointment, was easily confirmed, and arrived in Moscow on May 5, 1952. Things went badly from the beginning. In a June 18 letter to the State Department, he warned that damage was being done to his mission by US military intelligence-gathering agencies that were exploiting their diplomatic status for the purpose of collecting information on the Soviet military. He intended, therefore, to issue orders to all members of the mission to comply strictly with Soviet laws and regulations. Two months later he informed President Truman,

"We are so cut off and hemmed in with restrictions and ignored by the Soviet Government that it is as though no diplomatic relations existed at all."

He was not, then, in a good mood when, in September, he set out for a London conference of US ambassadors serving in Europe. On the way, the plane carrying him made a stop at Berlin's Tempelhof airport, where he was besieged by reporters, one of whom asked if he had many social contacts with Russians. Kennan snapped back: "I was interned here in Germany for several months during the last war. The treatment we receive in Moscow is just about like the treatment we internees received then, except that in Moscow we are at liberty to go out and walk the streets under guard." Almost immediately, the Soviet government declared him persona non grata. Shortly after the 1952 election of Gen. Dwight D. Eisenhower as president of the United States, the new secretary of state, John Foster Dulles, summoned Kennan to Washington to inform him that there was no place for him in the State Department or the Foreign Service.

Having failed to receive a new appointment within the required three months, Kennan was retired automatically in June 1953. Writing from the farm he had purchased in East Berlin, Pennsylvania, he observed that it was not until then that his retirement seemed really to begin. He wondered what lay ahead. Only, it seemed, three things: "solitude, depth of thought, and writing. And since all of these things were best achieved by addressing one's self to the third, then the great dictate seemed to be: to sit at a desk and write. The thoughts will come—they always do."

Kennan returned to the IAS, his working home for the rest of his life—with one brief return to government service. In the fall of 1960, John F. Kennedy won election to the presidency, and among his first official acts was a call Kennan to offer him an ambassadorship in Poland or Yugoslavia. Kennan chose the latter, pleased to be asked to serve one more time. He represented his country in the multiethnic Balkan land from 1961 to 1963, and although he enjoyed his time there, added Serbo-Croatian to his list of language proficiencies, and got on well with Marshal Tito, he found himself in constant conflict with a poorly informed and interfering Congress. In July 1963, he resigned and returned to the IAS, his career in the Foreign Service at a definitive end.

Kennan's favorite writer was Anton Chekhov, whose biographer he once aspired to be. In his judgment, the Russian viewed his mission as that of illuminating the deeper tragedy and irony of human existence. Yet "he never lost the love of life. To him, such things as beauty and laughter and conviviality and good food and the joy of creativity never paled." He was also intrigued by the fact that, while achieving fame for his stories and plays, Chekhov continued to pursue an active career in medicine. In a letter to his publisher, the great writer had declared that medicine was his lawful wife and literature his mistress.

Similarly, one can say that Kennan's lawful wife was diplomacy, and writing his mistress. As he once told his sister Jeanette, he could take more pride in one page of decent writing than in being an ambassador. During his brief tenure as ambassador to the USSR, he visited Yasnaya Polyana, Leo Tolstoy's estate. As he later wrote, "[There I felt] close to a world to which, I always thought, I could really have belonged, had circumstances permitted— belonged much more naturally and wholeheartedly than to the world of politics and diplomacy into which Fate had thrust me."

During his long years abroad Kennan certainly seized every opportunity to develop his literary skills—the edited version of his diaries runs to nearly seven hundred pages. But even when drafting government reports, he strove for beauty of expression. In September 1944, for example, he gave Averell Harriman a paper on Stalin, the Soviet Union, and the coming postwar era. He was wounded when his boss offered no response, but that was not the worst of it. "I did think," he confessed in his memoirs, "he might have observed, if he thought so, that it was well written." When he finally settled in at the IAS, Kennan was able to dedicate all of his time to writing—members do not have teaching responsibilities. He joined the School of Historical Studies primarily because he viewed historical writing as a branch of literature—both Winston Churchill and Theodor Mommsen, he pointed out, had won the Nobel Prize in *Literature.*

Although he tried to write history as literature, Kennan recognized that historians were necessarily limited to dealing with the external personalities of their subjects. "It is," he wrote in an essay on history as literature, "with the intimate undercurrent of men's lives that the true literary artist is permitted to deal, and does deal, in his greatest moments: with the inner souls of men rather than with what Freud has called their *personæ.*" At the same time, such an artist opened a window into his own soul—and for precisely that reason Kennan's diaries and memoirs meant even more to him than his histories or political writings. It was in those works that he revealed a truth about himself that he had discovered when he entered the Foreign Service: "Like the actor on the stage, I have been able, all my life, to be of greater usefulness to others by what, seen from a certain emotional distance, I seemed to be than by what, seen closely, I really was."

What understanding of his true self did Kennan obtain from his autobiographical writings, and to a lesser extent from his histories?

For one thing, he found that he was a man of the eighteenth, not the twentieth, century. "I am an eighteenth-century person," he told George Urban. "I'm persuaded that those of our forefathers who had their roots really back in the eighteenth century had more convincing values and better tastes than those whose roots were in the society that issued from the Industrial Revolution."

In one of the lectures he gave in Bad Nauheim, Kennan called his students' attention to a parallel between Russian and American history. In both lands, he pointed out, European culture of the eighteenth century had planted deep roots. It was, in fact, that culture for which many Americans felt nostalgic: the dignity; the simplicity; the respect for form; the polished, classical erudition; the acceptance of a clear stratification of society.

But there was more. In a 2000 interview he granted to the *New Yorker*, Kennan observed that, "If you look at the eighteenth century of Europe, there were injustices galore, but there were limits." Edward Gibbon was right, he believed, to list among the elements of strength in the European civilization of the eighteenth century the fact that the armies of the European powers were "exercised in temperate and indecisive conflicts." He had read Gibbon's *The History of the Decline and Fall of the Roman Empire* on transatlantic flights during the war and became persuaded that, as the great historian had written, "the decline of Rome was the natural and inevitable effect of immoderate greatness."

To his diaries Kennan confided that he had been profoundly influenced not only by Gibbon but by other eighteenth-century thinkers, such as Edmund Burke, Alexis de Tocqueville (an eighteenth-century mind), and the authors of *The Federalist Papers*, especially Alexander Hamilton. Kennan drew inspiration from the Founding Fathers not least because they "saw Americans as essentially no different from the general run of human beings: subject to the same limitations; affected by the same restrictions of vision; tainted by the same original sin or, in a more secular view, by the same inner conflicts between flesh and spirit, between self-love and charity." Not for them the latter-day doctrine of "American Exceptionalism," according to which, as Richard M. Weaver wrote, "the United States is somehow exempt from the past and present fate, as well as from many of the necessities, of other nations. Ours is a special creation, endowed with special immunities. As a kind of millennial state, it is not subject to the trials and divisions that have come upon others through time and history."

His father, Kennan told his own children, had grappled agonizingly with the trials and dilemmas of original sin. That inheritance was strengthened in him by the writings of Reinhold Niebuhr, to whose perceptions and thinking he declared himself to be more indebted than to those of any other person of his time. Unlike most liberal Protestants, Niebuhr could not shake his belief in man's sinful nature. To this belief he gave expression in the Gifford Lectures that he delivered in Edinburgh in 1939–40. In the modern liberal Protestant interpretation of Christianity, Niebuhr wrote in the published version of his lectures, "the problem of sin is not understood at all."

In Niebuhr's view, liberal Protestants had accommodated themselves too readily to modern culture's optimism concerning human nature. In opposition to that optimism, he set Christian realism, a view of man that, though eschewing despair and acknowledging the good of which men were capable, took seriously their capacity for evil. That capacity was a result of original sin, which Niebuhr did not understand as an inheritance from Adam or a factor that relieved men of their responsibility. It was each man's identity with Adam's nature that made sin inevitable—yet not necessary.

Kennan was particularly struck by *The Irony of American History*, in which Niebuhr observed that even the best human actions involve some guilt and that Americans deceived themselves by believing that they could act as tutors to mankind. Unable or unwilling to confront the ironies of their own history—virtues that too easily became vices, strengths that became weaknesses, wisdom that became folly—they refused to recognize the limits proper to finite beings. "The ironic elements in American history can be overcome," Niebuhr concluded, "only if American idealism comes to terms with the limits of all human striving, the fragmentariness of all human wisdom, the precariousness of all historic configurations of power, and the mixture of good and evil in all human virtue." Kennan could have written those words himself.

In Freudianism, Kennan discovered what he described as a secular version of original sin, namely that men are driven primarily by instincts (especially the urgings of sex and the impulses of aggression) that must, to a significant degree, be repressed if civilization is to be maintained; doing so, however, leads to frustration and existential discontent. That was the burden of Freud's *Das Unbehagen in der Kultur* (literally "Discomfort in Civilization," but translated as *Civilization and Its Discontents*). Human beings will always, Kennan told one interviewer, "feel a grave *Unbehagen*, a discomfort, at having to live in a civilized framework, and kick against it."

What all of this meant, according to Kennan, was that there is a tragic dimension to the human condition—tragic because the conflict between sin/instinct and civilized behavior was incurable. It was primarily that tragic sense that drew him closer to

Christianity, albeit in a decidedly personal form. When the *New Yorker* interviewer asked him why he was so strongly attracted to the historic faith, he replied that it recognized in the human condition the same element of tragedy that he recognized. That did not mean that he thought life not worth living; quite the contrary. In a draft for a lecture that he wrote in 1964, he pointed out that life could be full of excitement, beauty, and mystery. So great were those attractions that it was a profound experience even to live tragically—so much so that he wondered if it could ever be so profound if it were not tragic.

In common with many of his peers, Kennan concerned himself little with religious questions while at university or during his early years in the Foreign Service. Things began to change, however, when he went to Russia. He felt nothing but disgust for Soviet efforts to substitute a pagan for a Christian sacramental life, and he became aware, for the first time, of his own dependence on the latter. He sometimes attended the Russian Orthodox Church's Divine Liturgy, and on one occasion he visited the Pskovo-Pechorsky Orthodox Monastery (then in Estonia).

Princeton professor Arthur Link, the leading expert on Woodrow Wilson and a personal friend, had this to say of Kennan: "He was reared a Presbyterian, but he's been much more influenced by Russian Orthodoxy: the acceptance of things as they are, without getting too high expectations; [the view] that the world is fundamentally evil and that really there's not a great deal that you can do about it." Kennan himself put it this way in a talk he gave at Princeton's Trinity Episcopal Church on January 12, 1992: "[The central appeal of the Orthodox Faith] is the full-throated refrain 'God, have mercy.' *Gospodi pomilui.* And by this they mean: Lord, be kind to us. We know we are not perfect; we know our weaknesses. We are poor devils; we don't see all things clearly. Don't expect too much from us. But you know our sufferings. Be indulgent of us; treat us better than we deserve."

The Russian Orthodox Church did not, however, maintain a significant presence in the United States of Kennan's time. More important, as he told one of his biographers (Anders Stephanson), his life and character were stamped by his Presbyterian origins, and respect for his forebears made it difficult for him to think of himself any other way. During his time in Yugoslavia he often conducted Protestant services for embassy personnel, and in later years he spoke regularly to churches in Princeton. Five years before his death in 2005, he told the *New Yorker* interviewer that he had plans to set out his religious views in a privately printed book. He did complete a letter to his children in which he presented those views in broad outline. Not surprisingly, he emphasized that some of the most compelling of Christ's appeals were his efforts to persuade men of the dangers of self-love and of the need for a recognition of one's weaknesses.

With respect to God the Father, whom he referred to as the "Primary Cause," Kennan was essentially an eighteenth-century Deist. Having brought the universe into being and laid down the laws according to which it would operate, the Primary Cause promptly withdrew. It did not, in response to petitions from human beings, interfere in the workings of the laws it had established; to the travails of men it remained supremely indifferent. Concerning the divinity of Jesus, Kennan would say no more than that when a dream is a great and noble one, and when it is lived through with the devotion that marked Jesus's belief in his godlike identity, it ceases to be entirely a dream and becomes a reality. For Kennan, "God" meant the "Holy Spirit" (the "Comforter"). This "Merciful Deity,"

Kennan said, "[is] infused with understanding of and sympathy for our situation, involved as we are in the conflict between our physical and our spiritual natures, and prepared to give us such assistance as we deserve and can accept." Perhaps because Kennan was conscious of the fact that this was an unorthodox version of Christianity, he closed his letter to his children by identifying the Lord's Prayer, which he prayed every evening as a child, as the clearest expression of his faith.

2

For a Mature Foreign Policy

In 1951, Kennan delivered the Charles R. Walgreen Foundation Lectures at the University of Chicago; University of Chicago Press released them as *American Diplomacy, 1900–1950*. At the outset of that series of six lectures, he informed members of his audience that his organizing concept stemmed "from no abstract interest in history for history's sake . . . but from a preoccupation with the problems of foreign policy we have before us today." He was, in other words, drawn to history because he believed that the past contained important lessons for the present; from that approach to the record of the past he would never deviate.

Kennan's initial lecture, on the Spanish-American War of 1898, was a case in point. The war signaled a sea change in US foreign policy—from nonintervention to intervention, from principled restraint to crusading zeal. In 1895, as Kennan pointed out, Cuban insurgents renewed their struggle against Spanish rule. The cause of *Cuba libre* aroused the sympathies of the American people, but William McKinley, who assumed the office of president in 1897, was not initially inclined to intervene. "I have been through one war," he told a friend. "I have seen the dead piled up, and I do not want to see another." During the Civil War he served with the Twenty-Third Ohio Infantry and came under heavy fire when bringing rations to men on the line at Antietam.

The president was, however, under increasing pressure from William Randolph Hearst's *New York Journal* and Joseph Pulitzer's *New York World* to take action, especially after the battleship USS *Maine*, in Havana Harbor to protect American citizens, exploded (the cause is still unknown) and sank on February 15, 1898, with the loss of 266 American lives. It was that pressure, rather than any stubborn belligerence on the part of Spain, that finally led McKinley to change his mind. On April 20, Congress resolved that the United States demand that Spain withdraw its land and naval forces from Cuba and authorized the president to enforce the resolution, by force if necessary. This despite the fact, as Kennan noted, that measures short of war had not been exhausted. Given three days to comply with the ultimatum, Spain declared war on the United States on April 24. The United States returned the favor the following day and achieved a quick victory with little effort or loss of life—but that was far from being the end of it.

On May 1, Commodore George Dewey's Asiatic Squadron sailed into Manila Bay and destroyed the Spanish fleet; McKinley then dispatched soldiers to occupy Luzon, largest of the Philippine islands. Why? It seems, Kennan told his Chicago listeners, that Dewey's victory thrilled and pleased the American public. Yet in ending Spanish authority, the president faced the problem of replacing it and of breaking Filipino resistance, at a cost of twenty thousand Filipino and over four thousand American lives. By the terms of the Treaty of Paris (December 10, 1898), Spain renounced claims to Cuba (it became a US protectorate under the 1901 Platt Amendment), ceded Guam and Puerto Rico, and transferred sovereignty over the Philippines for $20 million.

Taking part in the treaty negotiations was McKinley's secretary of state, John Hay, who had acted as President Abraham Lincoln's private secretary before working for the *New York Tribune*, holding various diplomatic posts in Europe, and serving as assistant secretary of state. He was the US ambassador to the United Kingdom when the president chose him to replace William R. Day as secretary of state on September 30, 1898. Unlike Day, Hay supported the imperialistic terms of peace with Spain and, a year later, promoted the Open Door Policy, which aimed to obviate divisive spheres of influence in China and to secure that country's territorial and administrative integrity. Kennan devoted his second Chicago lecture to an analysis and criticism of that policy.

Hay acted as a result of a request made by Alfred Hippisley, an Englishman who worked for the Chinese Maritime Customs Service, a tax collection service that grew to include postal administration, harbor and waterway management, and antismuggling operations. He urged the United States to obtain assurances from European powers that they would not interfere with treaty ports in spheres of influence where the Customs Service had its establishments. Knowing little of the Far East, Hay turned to William Woodville Rockhill, soon to be the ambassador to China. Rockhill drafted a memorandum, on the basis of which a note was drawn up that Hay signed and circulated to Russia, Britain, Germany, France, Japan, and Italy on September 6, 1899.

The Rockhill note went beyond what Hippisley had asked; it contained a refusal on the part of the United States to recognize spheres of influence. According to Kennan, the reception accorded the note by the several powers was tepid. Nevertheless, Hay announced on March 20, 1900, that he had received satisfactory assurances from all the powers and that he regarded them as final and definitive. On that basis, the American public concluded that the United States had achieved a resounding diplomatic success, the assertion of American principles in international society.

At about the same time, the Boxer Rebellion, a violent antiforeigner and anti-Christian uprising, had thrown China temporarily into anarchy, and Hay circulated a second note. That one, dated July 3, 1900, stated that the policy of the United States was to seek to preserve Chinese territorial and administrative integrity. That seemed to commit the United States to the protection of China against foreign encroachments on her territory, but as Kennan pointed out it had little effect. In fact, when Japan, alarmed by Russian moves in Manchuria, asked if the United States would be willing to join in using force to assure observance of the principles it had enunciated, Hay replied that the United States was "not at present prepared to attempt singly, or in concert with other Powers, to enforce these views in the east by any demonstration which could present a character of hostility to any other Power." There was the awkward fact, too, that the United States had set up a regime in the Philippines that was in conflict with the Open Door principle.

Kennan did not blame Hay for his role in the entire misguided policy. In fact, he praised him as a great American gentleman who worked within a framework of government that was unsuitable for the conduct of foreign affairs of a great power. The lesson to be learned, according to Kennan, was that the self-righteous proclamation of high-minded principles could not replace a forthright balancing of power. He was to repeat that lesson on many other occasions.

On May 4, 1902, at the opening of Arlington National Cemetery, President Theodore Roosevelt told those gathered that Americans had fought in the Philippines for the triumph of civilization over savagery and barbarism. The American Anti-Imperialist League, formed June 15, 1898, took issue with the president. Among its members were former president Grover Cleveland, industrialist Andrew Carnegie, philosopher John Dewey, Henry and William James, and Mark Twain. These men argued that the annexation of the Philippines signaled the abandonment of the ideals of self-government and nonintervention.

Without referring to the league by name, Kennan told his Chicago audience that those who opposed Roosevelt's "triumph" had good reason to ask "by what right we Americans . . . could assume the rights of empire over other peoples and accept them into our system, regardless of their own feelings, as subjects rather than as citizens." As a result of the reading on American diplomatic history he had been able to do while in government service, he recognized that the historical traditions of US foreign policy stood in clear opposition to such action. In his memoirs, he wrote that he "had been struck by the contrast between the lucid and realistic thinking of early American statesmen of the Federalist period and the cloudy bombast of their successors of later decades."

The Federalist period, roughly from 1789 to 1801, appealed to Kennan not only because it was of the eighteenth century but because of the foreign policy principles that the Federalists enunciated. President George Washington, a staunch Federalist by conviction, applied those principles in his every action. In 1792, the War of the First Coalition set Austria, Prussia, Sardinia, Great Britain, Spain, and the Netherlands against revolutionary France, with which the United States had a treaty of alliance (1778). Nevertheless, Washington proclaimed his country's neutrality. To those who protested that morality—fidelity to treaty obligations and gratitude for aid during the War of Independence—required that the United States enter the fray, Alexander Hamilton, secretary of the treasury and one of the authors of *The Federalist Papers*, offered a response.

"The rule of morality" Hamilton stated in "Pacificus Number IV" (July 10, 1793) "is in this respect not exactly the same between Nations as between individuals. The duty of making its own welfare the guide of its actions is much stronger upon the former than upon the latter; in proportion to the greater magnitude and importance of national compared with individual happiness, to the greater permanency of the effects of national than of individual conduct." He continued:

> Millions and for the most part future generations are concerned in the present measures of government: While the consequences of the private actions of an individual, for the most part, terminate with himself or are circumscribed within a narrow compass . . . . An individual may on numerous occasions meritoriously indulge the emotions of generosity and benevolence; not only without an eye to, but even at the expense of his own interest. But a nation can rarely be justified in pursuing a similar course; and when it does so ought to confine itself within much stricter bounds.

There are echoes of this rule in Washington's Farewell Address of September 19, 1796, coauthored by Hamilton. There the president defended his Proclamation of Neutrality with respect to the War of the First Coalition and counseled the nation "to steer clear of permanent alliances with any portion of the foreign world." America may, he added, "safely trust to temporary alliances for extraordinary emergencies." Thomas Jefferson agreed. In his March 4, 1801, inaugural address he identified one of the essential principles of the American government as that of "peace, commerce, and honest friendship with all nations, entangling alliances with none." That Kennan sympathized with that principle is evidenced by his objection to the use of the term *alliance* for commitments that had not been properly negotiated and ratified by the Senate. Such careless use of the language merely sowed confusion.

It was in the same, or a similar, vein that John Quincy Adams, then secretary of state, delivered a July 4, 1821, address to the House of Representatives. His remarks were prompted by the *Edinburgh Review*, which had asked what America had done for mankind. More specifically, its editors demanded to know why America had not intervened on behalf of the European revolutionary movements of the 1820s. Although he was to become the sixth president of the United States, it was as a diplomat that Adams served as a model for Kennan. Not only did he place the national interest at the center of his foreign policies but he served as the first US minister to Russia (1809–14).

Adams's wisdom and experience were on full display in his Fourth of July address. He defended his country's policy of noninterference in words that Kennan was to cite again and again: "Wherever the standard of freedom and Independence has been or shall be unfurled, there will her heart, her benedictions and her prayers be. But she goes not abroad, in search of monsters to destroy. She is the well-wisher to the freedom and independence of all. She is the champion and vindicator only of her own. She will commend the general cause by the countenance of her voice, and the benignant sympathy of her example."

Adams died on February 23, 1848, three weeks after the signing of the Treaty of Guadalupe Hidalgo had ended the two-year Mexican-American War. As the victor, the United States forced Mexico to cede a vast territory that became California, Nevada, Utah, most of Arizona, half of New Mexico, a part of western Colorado, and a small section of Wyoming; the Mexican government also agreed to relinquish its claim to Texas. This expansion went hand in hand with the ideology of Manifest Destiny, but it concerned only regions contiguous to the United States, which continued to remain free of entanglements overseas—until the Spanish-American War.

The year prior to the beginning of that war, President McKinley had named Theodore Roosevelt as assistant secretary of the Navy, a post he left in order to lead the "Rough Riders" (First United States Volunteer Cavalry), who achieved fame for their role in the Battle of San Juan Hill (July 1, 1898) near Santiago, Cuba. Largely as a result of his war heroics, Roosevelt won election as governor of New York and, in 1900, as vice president of the United States. He acceded to the presidency when Leon Czolgosz assassinated President McKinley on September 14, 1901.

Roosevelt was the first president to recognize the full implications of America's emergence as a great power. As Henry Kissinger wrote, he "started from the premise that the United States was a power like any other, not a singular incarnation of virtue. If its interests collided with those of other countries, America had the obligation to draw on its strength to prevail." For him, the key foreign policy principles were the national interest and the balance of power, the primary goal of which was not to prevent conflicts of interest but to limit their extent.

Having pledged in 1904 not to seek a third term in 1908, Roosevelt left the White House in March 1909, the same year that the progressive journalist Herbert Croly published *The Promise of American Life*, a book that the former president read with admiration, not least because of what Croly had to say about foreign policy. "A genuinely national policy must be based upon a correct understanding of the national interest in relation to those of its neighbors and associates," Croly wrote. "That American policy did obtain such a foundation during the early years of American history is to be traced to the sound political judgment of

Washington and Hamilton. Jefferson and the Republicans did their best for a while to persuade the American democracy to follow the dangerous course of the French democracy, and to base its international policy not upon the firm ground of national interest, but on the treacherous sands of international democratic propagandism."

Those sands became more treacherous after Thomas Woodrow Wilson won the presidential election of 1912. A former president of Princeton University and governor of New Jersey, Wilson was the anti-Roosevelt. For him, America's international role was messianic: to spread its principles throughout the world. He regarded democracy not simply as one among other forms of political arrangement, but as a universally valid civil religion. In direct contrast to Hamilton, he asserted, "We are at the beginning of an age in which it will be insisted that the same standards of conduct and of responsibility for wrong done shall be observed among nations and their governments that are observed among the individual citizens of civilized states."

Wilson spoke those words in his April 2, 1917, war message to Congress. However regrettable a military commitment might be, "the world must be made safe for democracy." In other words, the war against Germany was to be understood as ideological in nature. From that, a number of consequences flowed, all of which Kennan took note of. To begin with, war aims could no longer be limited in scope and could not therefore be achieved without total victory—this, despite the fact that on January 22 Wilson had called for a "peace without victory." Kennan told his Chicago audience that there was "no more dangerous delusion, none that has done us a greater disservice in the past or that threatens to do us a greater disservice in the future, than the concept of total victory."

That was not all. By attaching an absolute value to their cause, Americans began to view the United States as the seat of all virtue and the German enemy as the embodiment of all evil. The war, then, was no longer seen as a traditional struggle for power but as an apocalyptic confrontation. It was not that, according to Kennan, but it was the great catastrophe of Western civilization in the twentieth century, the worst consequence of which was World War II, which resulted in the deaths, military and civilian, of countless millions. In that horror, the Nazi regime, though not all Germans, was evil and there was no possibility of ending the war through negotiations with Hitler. As Kennan pointed out, however, the Allies' policy of unconditional surrender undercut a German resistance prepared to assassinate the Führer and submit to a negotiated surrender.

In the sixth and last of his Chicago lectures, Kennan spoke of the foreign policy lessons to be learned not only from America's participation in the world wars but from its relations with other countries since the Spanish-American War. Chief among them, in his view, was that the national interest alone should serve as diplomacy's guide: "We should have the modesty to admit that our own national interest is all that we are really capable of knowing and understanding—and the courage to recognize that if our purposes and undertakings here at home are decent ones, unsullied by arrogance or hostility toward other people or delusions of superiority, then the pursuit of our national interest can never fail to be conducive to a better world."

Not long after he delivered the Chicago lectures, Kennan left the Foreign Service (involuntarily) and began his long career as a permanent member of the Institute for Advanced Study's School of Historical Studies. It was only natural that he chose as the subject for his first work of historical scholarship the tangled web of Soviet-American relations. Nor is it surprising that he wrote his two-volume *Soviet-American Relations, 1917–1920* primarily as a tutorial regarding the proper—and improper—conduct of foreign policy. In a diary entry of August 14, 1950, he had written that "no one in my position can contribute to an understanding of US foreign policy unless he first turns historian, earns public confidence and respect on the study of an earlier day, and then gradually carries the public up to a clear and comprehensible view of the occurrences of these recent years."

Kennan's focus on America's ill-advised military intervention in postrevolutionary Russia served as a cautionary tale. In his view, diplomats, and the American people in general, would be wise to think long and hard before intervening in the internal affairs of foreign lands. The principal figure in his detailed reconstruction of the past was Woodrow Wilson, whom Kennan praised for his aversion to intervention in general and to intervening in Russia's internal politics in particular. Unfortunately, however, the president had never been in Russia and possessed little knowledge of Russian affairs.

More important, after Russia exited the war in March 1918, Wilson began to see reason in the Allies' concern that war supplies in Archangel and Vladivostok, supplies that they had provided, might fall into German hands. Fearing a German-Finnish attack on Murmansk—site of a new and relatively ice-free port not far distant from Archangel—a small British and French force went ashore. The Murmansk Soviet was dominated by Mensheviks (more moderate socialists) and Social Revolutionaries and pursued an independent course not unfriendly to the Allies; it offered no objection. What Kennan could not have known is that Lenin initially approved of the Allied landing for fear of losing the port to the German-Finnish force. Bolsheviks in control of Vladivostok did object, however, to the Japanese marines who landed in April after the murder on shore of three of their countrymen.

These were small and defensible actions, hardly an intervention that had as its aim the overthrow of Soviet power. But matters took a different turn as a result of the so-called Czech Legion, made up of Russian-born Czechs and Slovaks who had been serving in the Russian army and later of POWs who swelled the corps to sixty thousand men. Thanks to negotiations with Tomáš Masaryk, head of the Czechoslovak National Council, the Soviets granted the legion, now under the French High Command, permission to move via the Trans-Siberian Railway from Ukraine—it had fought in the Galician campaign of June 1917—to Vladivostok, whence Allied ships were to transport it around the world to France, where it would join in the struggle against Germany and Austria-Hungary. Uncertain as to the legionaries reliability, however, Commissar for Foreign Affairs Leon Trotsky demanded that they surrender their arms or be shot on the spot.

The Czecho-Slovaks refused to disarm, and after a violent clash with some Hungarian prisoners, they turned on local Soviet authorities investigating the incident. Soon hostilities between the legionaries and the Bolsheviks broke out all along the Trans-Siberian Railway line. Although the Czechs and Slovaks were the kind of little peoples for whom Wilson reserved a special sympathy, he initially resisted any call to intervene on their behalf—until he met Masaryk, who was, like him, a professor and a believer in democracy as a secular religion.

On July 6, 1918, Wilson called a White House meeting of his top advisers and set forth a series of propositions and a program of action. Having learned that the Czecho-Slovaks had succeeded in taking Vladivostok and declared the city an Allied protectorate, he stated that—"on sentimental grounds"—the United States and other governments were obligated to help them form a junction with their compatriots farther to the west. He therefore proposed the sending of seven thousand troops to Vladivostok, where they would join an equal number of Japanese troops (Japan actually sent seventy thousand). The two governments would announce publicly that their sole purpose was to aid the Czecho-Slovaks in their fight against German and Austrian prisoners—though the legionaries were actually fighting the Bolsheviks. That ill-informed decision ended whatever possibility there was of limited communication with the Bolshevik regime, communication that might have altered the subsequent course of Soviet-American relations.

Every bit as damaging as Wilson's decision to intervene was his disinclination to rely on the counsel of professional diplomats or to pursue his objectives through traditional diplomatic channels. If he sought any advice at all, it was from his confidant Col. Edward M. House, not from David Francis, whom he had named ambassador to Russia in 1916. To be sure, Francis was not a professional diplomat and, as Kennan pointed out, his assignment was made more difficult by the policy of nonrecognition of the Bolshevik regime, adopted primarily because the Bolsheviks sought to withdraw from the war. Kennan maintained that the nonrecognition policy was a mistake—a result of "the characteristic American concept of diplomatic representation as a gesture of friendship to peoples rather than a channel of communication among governments."

About nonprofessional figures who conducted semiofficial diplomacy on their own authority Kennan had a great deal to say. In particular he pointed to Raymond Robins, head of a Red Cross mission to Russia. Robins was a left-liberal who despised the tsarist government and was therefore sympathetic to the Soviet regime;

he was, in fact, in favor of giving it direct military aid so that it might continue to prosecute the war against Germany. Thanks in large measure to his constant companion Alexander Gumberg, a Soviet citizen—and, according to William Bullitt, a communist agent—Robins was able to move freely in Bolshevik circles. To his credit, in Kennan's view, he believed in the necessity of official contact with the Soviet authorities; moreover, he (like Kennan) rejected the widely held belief that the Bolsheviks were German agents.

At the same time, however, Robins was, in Kennan's opinion, the kind of irregular diplomat whom Washington should have discouraged. It is always unwise, he believed, to permit inexperienced people whose status is unclear to dabble in transactions between governments. That is why he chose to dedicate the second volume of his history, *The Decision to Intervene*, to the memory of "two members of America's Foreign Service, DeWitt Clinton Poole and Maddin Summers, of whose faithful and distinguished efforts in Russia on their country's behalf this volume gives only an incomplete account."

Summers, the consul general, strongly opposed Robins's meddling in affairs that should have remained in the hands of responsible authorities. He complained to Ambassador Francis that Robins undermined the work of the embassy and the consular service, and after a particularly bitter confrontation with the interloper he went home to rest and died, apparently of a brain hemorrhage, the following day. As his second-in-command, Poole assumed Summers's responsibilities and engaged in what appeared to be promising discussions with Georgy Chicherin, the scion of a distinguished family of the old regime who had succeeded Trotsky as commissar for foreign affairs. Kennan believed that, absent the

American decision to intervene, the exchanges between Poole and Chicherin might have developed into an orderly process of communication between the two governments. That may well have been wishful thinking, but it did teach the important lesson that diplomacy should always be conducted by those who are professionally trained.

We have seen that, for Kennan, the Great War was the great catastrophe of the twentieth century, the Bolshevik Revolution being only one of the disasters that flowed from it. At or near the top of the list of causes of that war was, in his judgment, a failure of diplomacy, to the history of which he resolved to set his hand. As in his study of Soviet-American relations, he hoped thereby to guide the decisions of contemporary statesmen and educate their peoples so as to prevent another, truly apocalyptic, conflict. On the basis of preliminary research and reflection, he arrived at the conclusion that the Franco-Russian alliance of 1894 was the most fateful diplomatic event on the road to war.

Kennan entitled his book *The Decline of Bismarck's European Order: Franco-Russian Relations, 1875–1890*, thereby signaling that his true subject was the great German statesman and consummate practitioner of Realpolitik. From 1864 to 1871, Otto von Bismarck provoked, fought, and won three wars—the last against France— but he projected a limited and realistic *political* objective, namely to create Germany as a more defensible Greater Prussia. Once having achieved his objective, he made an end to hostilities; never was he tempted to destroy his enemies utterly. In fact, he did not regard them as enemies, but as momentary obstacles in his political path. During the years 1871 to 1890, no one worked for peace in Europe with more skill and resolve than the Iron Chancellor. In this, as in other respects, he was, Kennan wrote in praise, "a man of the eighteenth century."

Bismarck was well aware that France's sense of humiliation was profound and that she recognized that she could not gain revenge by her own efforts; she needed an ally. Lying to the east of Germany, Russia was the obvious choice, even though *her* likely enemy was Austria-Hungary, not Germany. Moreover, monarchical Russia harbored a particular distaste for republican France. Those facts, together with his former experience as Prussian ambassador in Russia, persuaded Bismarck that Prussia/Germany had no fundamental interests in conflict with those of that country; Russian friendship, then, could be purchased for a minimal price. Even so, Tsar Alexander III, who ascended the throne upon the assassination of his father, Alexander II, adopted a critical view of Bismarck and the Germans, in part because of the influence of his Danish wife, who had neither forgotten nor forgiven Bismarck for Prussia's successful 1864 war against Denmark.

One who attempted to moderate the tsar's antagonism was Nikolai Karlovich Giers, the Russian foreign minister whom Kennan ranked second only to Bismarck among European diplomats of the second half of the nineteenth century. Of Swedish origin but thoroughly Russified, Giers sought to preserve peace with Germany and Austria-Hungary. He found, Kennan observed, an amicable relationship with the Germans not merely useful but essential to Russia's security.

Amicable relations between Russia and Germany seemed to be solidified by the secret Reinsurance Treaty, signed on June 18, 1887. According to its terms, the countries were to observe a benevolent neutrality in the event that one of them became involved in a war with a third party. If, however, Germany attacked France or Russia attacked Austria-Hungary the provision would not apply. Unfortunately for the future of Europe, Kaiser Wilhelm II forced Bismarck to resign on March 18, 1890, and, shortly thereafter, his successor, Count Leo von Caprivi, allowed the treaty to lapse. With it, according to Kennan, disappeared the last formal impediment to a closer military-political relationship between Russia and France.

Bismarck had negotiated the treaty as part of a plan to obfuscate the relations between European governments to such an extent that no nation bent on aggression could know in advance what, or how many, enemies it would have to confront. That constituted genius of the sort that Kennan hoped would serve as a model for America's diplomats. The latter might find it difficult or impossible to keep as many balls in the air as Bismarck could, but they might at least follow him by ruling out actions based on personal prejudices. "I cannot," Bismarck once observed, "reconcile personal sympathies and antipathies toward foreign powers with my sense of duty in foreign affairs; indeed I see in them the embryo of disloyalty toward the Sovereign and the country I serve."

Although he found it necessary to show deference to the tsar's prejudices, Nikolai Giers inclined to the same view. He may have been thought colorless and timid by more high-powered figures around the Russian court, but Bismarck, a man not easily impressed by foreign statesmen, thought highly of him. For his part, Kennan believed that the Russian could serve as another model for American diplomats—not least because of "his long and faithful adherence to the principles of restraint and conciliation in his dealings with the representatives of the other Powers."

In summing up his admiration for the Russian, Kennan wrote that "intellectually, and in mastery of the subject matter and methodology of the diplomacy of the time, Giers was not inferior to Bismarck. . . . Whoever concerns himself extensively with the diplomatic documents of the period will not be able to escape the conclusion that the record of European diplomacy in the second half of the nineteenth century contains the name of no more competent professional diplomatist and statesman, and of none who was more devoted to the preservation of peace."

Too few of Giers's opposite numbers and of the European peoples shared that devotion. In the years following Bismarck's dismissal from office they came increasingly to regard war as inevitable, while at the same time contemplating the prospect lightheartedly. They failed to take into account changes in the technology of warfare that would render individual valor all but meaningless. After two world wars and millions of lost lives, Kennan concluded, the lesson should be clear—in an age of nuclear weapons, war was suicidal: "[If that truth] can be reinforced by the examination of the mistakes and bewilderments of political leaders acting nearly a hundred years ago, then even the length and detail of this portion of a study of the Franco-Russian alliance will not have lacked their justification."

In *The Fateful Alliance: France, Russia, and the Coming of the First World War*, Kennan continued his study. He provided a detailed account of the meetings that took place between Russian general-adjutant Nikolai Obruchev and French general Raoul le Mouton de Boisdeffre. On August 18, 1892, the two men signed a military convention that constituted the basis for the Franco-Russian alliance. It stipulated that if France were to be attacked by Germany, or by Italy supported by Germany, Russia would attack Germany. If Russia were to be attacked by Germany, or by Austria-Hungary supported by Germany, France would attack Germany. In the event that the Triple Alliance (concluded in 1882) or one of its signatories (Germany, Austria-Hungary, or Italy) should mobilize, France and Russia would immediately do the same.

Kennan told the story with skill and eloquence, following the lead of Harold Nicolson, the British diplomat, literary biographer, diarist, and diplomatic historian, whom he met in Berlin around 1930. Nicolson was, he told John Lukacs, his "master and teacher in the writing of diplomatic history." As in his earlier histories, however, Kennan was primarily interested in the lessons to be learned from its telling. The alliance, he observed, "was a purely military document. Nothing was said in it about the political objectives for which one might be fighting." Here he was drawing on the wisdom of Carl von Clausewitz, who famously asserted in *On War*, that "war is nothing but the continuation of politics with the admixture of other means." The German believed that war, to be justified, had to serve realistic political goals. "The political object is the goal," he wrote, "war is the means of reaching it, and means can never be considered in isolation from their purposes."

To formulate objectives would be—as it was in the dynastic wars of the eighteenth century—to set limits, but World War I was limitless in its aims, which was another way of saying that the only aim was the total destruction of the enemy—and hence total war. It was, Kennan wrote, "in this primitive spirit that the great powers were to enter upon World War I. It was in the same spirit that they would fight World War II to the end."

In an essay entitled "Flashbacks" that the *New Yorker* published the year after *The Fateful Alliance* appeared, Kennan reflected on the rewards of writing about the history of the pre–World War I years and the first years of Bolshevik rule. He had come to know the heroes and antiheroes of his work as though they were contemporaries, knowing as they could not know, that they were all actors in a tragic drama. He hoped to have communicated that to contemporary politicians and diplomats, for he believed that he had perceived in records of the past lessons that could help to identify hopeful roads into the future and to refrain from entering on paths at the end of which there is no hope.

Kennan never wrote the projected third volume of his diplomatic history, which would have taken the story from 1894 to the Soviet regime's withdrawal from the war. In part that was because of his advancing age; he turned eighty in 1984, the year that Pantheon Books published *The Fateful Alliance*. For that work he had conducted research in the Archives des affairs étrangères at the Quai d'Orsay in Paris; the Haus-, Hof-, und Staatsarchiv in Vienna; the Arkhiv Vneshnei Politiki in Moscow; the Public Record Office in London; and the Overhofmarskallatetarkiv and Foreign Office archives in Copenhagen. He was physically not up to another round of research of that kind.

There was, to be sure, another reason why he left his history uncompleted—the demands on his time as a public and academic lecturer. Often burdensome, they provided different opportunities to offer foreign policy lessons. Among the most important lessons he taught as a lecturer was that conducting a mature foreign policy presented a particular challenge for democratic governments. A close student of Alexis de Tocqueville's *Democracy in America*, Kennan borrowed the Frenchman's words in the published version of Oxford lectures he delivered in 1957–58. The Paris Peace Conference of 1919 demonstrated that, in the relations between nations, "a democracy can only with great difficulty regulate the details of an important undertaking, persevere in a fixed design, and work out its execution in spite of serious obstacles."

One reason for that unsteadiness of purpose was that those charged with responsibility for the conduct of a democratic foreign policy had to contend with public opinion, which was woefully uninformed and notoriously erratic. In general, domestic politics intruded too much on their ability to act in the national interest. It was sometimes easier, Kennan told a Princeton audience in 1954, for an authoritarian government to shape its external conduct in an enlightened manner than it was for a democratic government locked in domestic political conflict. That echoed what Tocqueville had observed, namely that it was in the nature of democracies to decide questions of foreign policy on purely domestic considerations.

In view of the handicaps under which diplomats in a democracy had to labor, Kennan argued that it behooved them to recognize that there exist problems in the world that Americans could not solve, global dilemmas that would have to find their solution without US involvement. At the very least they should refuse to answer the siren call to spread democracy around the world. As we have seen, that crusader impulse can be traced back to Woodrow Wilson's dream of a world made safe for democracy. Henceforth that messianic goal, not Washington's Farewell Address, was to be the lodestar of American foreign policy; all of Wilson's successors have shared his prophetic vision.

Of Franklin Roosevelt, for example, Gen. Charles de Gaulle observed that he viewed international democracy as a kind of universal remedy. Republican presidents were equally intoxicated by democratic spirits. Henry Kissinger reported that on his first day in office President Richard Nixon, a realist in outlook, had nonetheless called for Woodrow Wilson's desk and used it while he was in the Oval Office. In his address to the British Parliament in 1982, President Ronald Reagan called for an international campaign for democracy.

Writing in opposition to that crusading spirit, Kennan pointed out that "democracy" was a notoriously loose term. "Many varieties of folly and injustice contrive to masquerade under this designation. . . . There can be tyrannies of a majority as well as tyrannies of a minority, with the one hardly less odious than the other. Hitler came into power . . . with an electoral mandate, and there is scarcely a dictatorship of this age that would not claim the legitimacy of mass support."

In any event, democracy, as Americans understood it, was not necessarily the future of all mankind, nor was it the duty of the US government to assure that it became that. Most governments, past and present, were nondemocratic, products in most cases of the unique historical experience of a people and a region. Kennan was not prepared to condemn every one of them. With Edmund Burke, he reprobated no form of government merely on abstract principles.

Kennan lived long enough to witness crusades for democracy become intertwined with those for "human rights," imagined by many to be the world's religion and said to belong to all human beings simply by virtue of their being human. Human rights advocates do not say merely that certain rights should belong to all people in all places at all times; that might be a proper matter for discussion or debate. Instead they insist that certain rights already belong to all people, whether or not particular governments recognize and embody them in positive law.

It is more than passing odd that great thinkers of the past such as Plato and Aristotle failed to recognize the existence of human rights. Historian Lynn Hunt asked pointedly how rights could be universal if they are not universally recognized. The distinguished contemporary philosopher Alasdair Macintyre compared belief in human rights to belief in witches and unicorns. Undeterred, the General Assembly of the United Nations on December 10, 1948, approved and issued *The Universal Declaration of Human Rights,* which asserts, among other remarkable claims, that everyone possesses rights "to rest and leisure, including reasonable limitation of working hours and periodic holidays with pay" and "to a standard of living adequate to the health and well-being of himself and of his family, including food, clothing, housing and medical care and necessary social services."

Are these rights, Kennan asked in disbelief, "really to be without obligation on the beneficiary's part? Is he really to be at liberty to spend his life going fishing, or taking his ease in other ways, and still be entitled to demand that he be provided with all these things that Article 25 assures to him? And if so, who is supposed to pay for them?" Although he could understand human rights as ideal projections of Western liberal principles, he could not conceive of them as already existing in the absence of a granting authority, an enforcing agency, and a set of corresponding duties.

The idea of rights remote from human authorship, Kennan confessed, led him into "philosophical thickets"; alone the abundant contradictions among the alleged human rights sufficed to arouse his skepticism. Were there but a single human right, the concept would at least be coherent, but because there are said to be a great many—and the list continues to grow—conflicts are inevitable, whereupon a human decision regarding precedence will be required. But that takes us back to human authorship.

This confusion makes it difficult, if not impossible, to make sense of anxious criticisms of the human rights record of this or that government. Early in 1990, Kennan attended a dinner in honor of George Shultz and was struck by the former secretary of state's stress, in his after-dinner speech, on the alleged success of the US government in persuading or compelling other governments to respect human rights. It grated on his sensibilities as a historian. Writing in the 1990s, he recalled what he had said about the Open

Door principles in his Walgreen Lectures. "The mere fact that we had stated these admirable principles, and had demanded respect for them, and had done so in ways that would allow our government to appear in noble posture before world and American opinion, was felt to be quite enough. . . . The reader will forgive me if I sense a certain whiff of this same sanctimoniousness in American statements and demands about human rights."

Kennan's reflections on democracy and human rights went hand in hand with his broader efforts to persuade his countrymen that conducting foreign policy was a practical, not a moral, exercise. In 1985, he elaborated on the brief remarks on that subject that he had made in the Walgreen Lectures. The core of his argument was this: "Government is an agent, not a principal. Its primary obligation is to the *interests* of the national society it represents, not to the moral impulses that elements of that society may experience." Put another way, as "thinkers as far apart in time as Alexander Hamilton and Reinhold Niebuhr" noted, "morality is not the same thing for an individual, responsible only to himself, as it is for a government, trustee for the interests of others."

Views such as those did not mean that Kennan was an immoralist; far from it. He made that clear in a letter to John Lukacs, dated September 6, 1956:

> I do indeed believe in morals, but as a matter of individual faith, conscience, and principles. What I detest is moralistic posing and the attempt to clothe in the garments of virtue functions and undertakings that are very much a product of the ambitions and appetites and necessities of this world. While a Presbyterian, I fear that I share in high degree the ancient Christian principle that the worldly power—Caesar—has nothing to do with the Kingdom of God. In any case,

I regard the role of government as something irrelevant to Christian ethics, and greatly dislike seeing the exercise of world power (and foreign policy is only a part of this) masked as a spiritual purpose.

Those who clamor for foreign interventions on moral grounds assume, mistakenly, that there exist universally recognized standards of morality. What they are actually demanding, according to Kennan, is that the target of their displeasure act in accordance with *their* standards, those rooted in America's national and religious traditions. Interventionists rarely stop to consider the possible consequences of forcing on a foreign government their notions of moral behavior or, worse, of conspiring in its overthrow. There is always, to begin with, the problem of a viable alternative. And even if a ready force waits in the wings, one can never be certain that it will bring about an improvement in conditions. All in all, he thought it best to respect "the sound old principle" of noninterference in the domestic affairs of other countries.

It should be clear by now that Kennan recommended to US diplomats and to the American people a foreign policy devoid of messianic tendencies and of any belief that the United States has answers to everybody else's problems: "We Americans must realize that we cannot be the keepers and moral guardians of all the peoples in this world. We must become more modest, and recognize the necessary limits to the responsibility we can assume." Or as he explained to his friend Louis Halle, "We are not under any obligation to practice charity toward others on a major scale, or to 'develop' them, or to try to reform their political habits, or to restrain them from violence. We may find it desirable, in the pursuit of our own reasonable interests, to do all these things; but we are under no obligation to others to do any of them."

A mature foreign policy would be restrained and cognizant of the realities of power in the relations between states. Such realities, Kennan argued in his Chicago lectures, should be accepted "without feeling the obligation of moral judgment, to take them as existing and inalterable human forces, neither good or bad, and to seek their point of maximum equilibrium rather than their reform or their repression." He returned to those realities repeatedly, often in unconcealed exasperation with those who refused to recognize or respect them. "They will soon seep into any legalistic structure which we erect to govern international life," he told his diary on August 4, 1944. "They will permeate it. They will become the content of it, and the structure will remain only the form." In *Around the Cragged Hill*, he put it more concisely: "Government always implies and involves power."

In this understanding, Kennan aligned himself closely with Hans Morgenthau, a leading realist whom he had invited to act as a consultant to the Policy Planning Staff. In *In Defense of the National Interest*—which also began as a series of Walgreen Lectures—the German-born student of international relations argued that the United States almost invariably mistook legal agreements and arrangements for realities. Hence the shock that Americans suffered when the Soviet Union violated the Yalta agreement, according to which democratic governments were to be established in Eastern Europe on the basis of free elections. He pointed out that Yalta was doomed from the beginning because the USSR was in military possession of the region. That fact overrode any idea of universal democracy.

Morgenthau was no more an exponent of Machiavellianism or cynicism than Kennan was. In a section of the same book entitled "The Moral Dignity of the National Interest," he wrote that the choice was not between moral principles and the national interest but between one set of moral principles divorced from political reality and another derived from that reality. To be meaningful in an international context, moral principles, he argued, had to move from the abstract to the concrete; what they required could not be decided on without constant reference to the circumstances on which they were being brought to bear. There being no universally recognized moral code, it was incumbent on each state to frame its moral judgments with an eye to protecting its—that is, its citizens'—vital interests and indeed its very existence. Such a view argued for moderation and ruled out moral crusades.

Because he shared views such as these, Kennan advocated a balance-of-power rather than a legalistic approach to international problems. According to the latter, problems could be solved on the basis of legal or contractual provisions laid down and accepted in advance. Kennan instanced in that regard international law, the League of Nations, the United Nations, and the Kellogg-Briand Pact (1928) that renounced war as an instrument of national policy. Although he had no objection to efforts to encourage the rule of law in international life, he maintained that power would always trump it. To pretend otherwise was to invite misunderstanding and court disaster.

3

Russia and Eastern Europe

Kennan's foreign policy principles formed the basis for his counsel regarding particular problems. First among them, of course, was the Cold War with Soviet Russia. We have seen how he viewed relations, or the lack of them, with the Bolshevik regime from 1917 to 1920. When, finally, President Roosevelt established formal relations in 1933, Kennan, fluent in Russian, was among the first members of the Foreign Service sent to Moscow. Unlike so many of his generation of Americans, he was never attracted to Marxist ideology. "I have never," he told John Lukacs, "had anything but contempt for the philosophic shallowness of the Marxists, who ignore the individual, subjective dimension of human tragedy and believe that everything could be put to rights by a bit of tinkering with the social relationships among bodies of men."

From the first, on the other hand, Kennan professed a profound admiration for the Russian people. That only deepened his hostility toward the regime under which they were forced to live. At its head was Stalin, a Georgian whose chief characteristics he immediately recognized as being "an inordinate touchiness, an endless vindictiveness, an inability ever to forget an insult or a slight, but great patience and power of dissimulation in selecting and preparing the moment to settle the score." Cordial relations with such a man and such a regime were not possible, but that did not mean, according to Kennan, that channels of communication should not be kept open.

When Kennan returned to Moscow in 1944, Soviet-American relations had improved—far too much in his opinion; too many of his countrymen, including President Roosevelt, believed that the wartime era of good feelings could and should continue. Thanks to the Long Telegram and the Mr. X essay, he was able to convince his superiors to adopt a policy of containment of the Soviet Union, a policy that was vindicated when, in 1991, the communist regime collapsed; but not before the policy was subjected to withering criticism. Former Trotskyite James Burnham, for one, thought containment too defensive and argued for the liberation of those under communist rule. Was that not a call for World War III? Kennan thought so.

The full significance of Stalin's death in 1953 seemed to Kennan to be lost on America and the West. In his judgment, containment immediately lost much, if not all, of its rationale. He did not mean to suggest that the Soviet Union had changed overnight, but he pointed out that Nikita Khrushchev, while certainly a communist, presided over a thaw, a dismantling of the Terror. It did not take much more than that to persuade his critics that the hawk had become a dove.

Kennan never thought in terms of hawks and doves, but of reality at specific times and places. Having been highly critical of the Soviet regime during his years of service in Moscow, he nevertheless recognized that even dictatorial regimes were subject to change—some for the better, some for the worse. He knew that during the war myths of the mild-mannered and self-effacing

Stalin—"Uncle Joe"—and the progressive Soviet regime had been propagated in the United States. These myths were fully on display in the film version of Joseph Davies's *Mission to Moscow*. Requested by Franklin Roosevelt and directed by Michael Curtiz, just coming off of *Casablanca* (1942), it was introduced by Davies, who opined that "no leaders of a nation have been so misrepresented and misunderstood as those in the Soviet government during those critical years between the two world wars." Those were the years of the Great Terror and the Moscow Trials, the victims of which were portrayed in the film as fifth columnists working for Germany and Japan.

With the end of the war and the Sovietization of Eastern Europe, American attitudes shifted rapidly and dramatically; wartime hope became postwar disillusionment. After the Soviet Union crushed the Hungarian Revolution in 1956, even some communists turned against it; talk of World War III was in the air. Such talk was in Kennan's estimation especially dangerous after the Soviets exploded a nuclear device in the summer of 1949. From the first he was convinced, with good reason, that a nuclear war would be the end of anything resembling a civilization. At the same time, he thought that America and the West exaggerated the Soviet military threat and were overly impressed by Soviet achievements when news arrived of the October 4, 1957, launching of Sputnik, the world's first artificial satellite.

It happened that news of Sputnik arrived on the eve of the first of Kennan's Reith Lectures. He had accepted an invitation to serve as the Eastman Professor at Balliol College, Oxford, for the 1957–58 academic year and, in conjunction, to deliver the prestigious series over the BBC; Bertrand Russell, Arnold Toynbee, and J. Robert Oppenheimer were previous lecturers. Kennan used the occasion to caution his listeners not to make too much of Sputnik.

The Kremlin rulers faced serious problems, not the least of which was an intelligentsia that was beginning to ask pointed questions. Nor should Soviet activity in underdeveloped countries occasion undue alarm. If some of those countries threatened to go communist unless they received Western aid, the West's answer should be "then go."

In two controversial lectures, Kennan urged the West to give up its unrealistic insistence that a unified Germany be free to join NATO; this, no Soviet government would countenance. In effect it would require that Soviet troops withdraw unilaterally from Central Europe. The Soviets had, however, indicated a willingness to discuss a mutual withdrawal of military forces from Europe's center; why not put their seriousness to the test? It would be preferable to the continuation of the nuclear arms race. As he did repeatedly in the years that remained to him, Kennan opposed so much as the thought of unleashing such weapons on Russia or any other country.

In the years from 1957 to the collapse of the USSR in 1991, Kennan intensified his efforts to encourage realistic diplomatic negotiations with the Soviet authorities and to discourage military, especially nuclear, competition. He considered the Nixon-Kissinger policy of détente to be an important step in the direction of improved Soviet-American relations. As secretary of state, Kissinger brought to that effort "a measure of imagination, boldness of approach, and sophistication of understanding without which it would have been difficult to achieve." Unfortunately, in Kennan's view, Watergate and Moscow's failure to live up to the 1975 Helsinki Accords' pledge to respect human rights emboldened antidétente forces, who were unduly fixated on the Soviet-US military rivalry.

The early 1980s offered Kennan little hope for improved Soviet-American relations; they were, in his judgment, in a dreadful and dangerous condition. After eighteen years as general secretary of the Communist Party of the Soviet Union, the sclerotic Leonid Brezhnev died on November 10, 1982. He was succeeded by Yuri Andropov, ambassador to Hungary during the Hungarian Revolution and former chairman of the KGB (who drank scotch and listened to jazz, according to an admiring Western media). He died on February 9, 1984, and was succeeded by the geriatric Konstantin Chernenko, who died on March 10, 1985. Neither of the latter was in office long enough to do more than maintain a crumbling status quo. On March 11, 1985, however, the much younger Mikhail Gorbachev assumed power and, according to Kennan, gave a dying system the coup de grâce it deserved. For the new Russian leader, Kennan's enthusiasm was unrestrained. Not only did he know how to conduct himself in the international arena but he was well-educated, urbane, intelligent, and persuasive.

If anything dampened Kennan's enthusiasm, it was the election of Ronald Reagan in 1980. He believed the new president and the administration he headed to be too belligerent, too persuaded that the Soviet leaders behaved properly only when confronted by superior military force, especially nuclear. By 1982, he had all but given up hope that the administration would be able to conduct serious and responsible negotiations with the USSR. When, in a speech of March 8, 1983, the president described the Soviet Union as an "evil empire," Kennan was even more certain that Soviet-American relations would continue to worsen and that the nuclear danger would increase.

It turned out that Kennan was wrong about the president, who shared his abhorrence of nuclear weapons. "For the eight years I was president," Reagan wrote in his memoirs, "I never let my dream of a nuclear-free world fade from my mind." Believing as he did that a nuclear war could not be won and that Mutual

Assured Destruction (MAD) was both immoral and unacceptably risky, he resolved to force negotiations in a new and more promising direction.

Like Kennan, Reagan believed that the Soviet Union faced serious problems, especially with respect to the economy. He reasoned that he could, by forcing the Soviets to engage in all-out competition, particularly in the sphere of military spending, bring them to recognize that it was in their interest to agree to substantive nuclear arms reductions. After the March 30, 1981, attempt on his life, he became even more determined to rid the world of nuclear weapons. "Perhaps having come so close to death," he wrote in his memoirs, "made me feel I should do whatever I could in the years God had given me to reduce the threat of nuclear war."

Reagan met Gorbachev in Geneva in November 1985 and again in Reykjavik, Iceland, in October 1986. The latter meeting ended without result because of a disagreement over Reagan's plans for the Strategic Defense Initiative, a system that could intercept and destroy ballistic missiles. Nevertheless, the president recognized that Gorbachev shared his desire to abolish nuclear weapons. When they met in Washington in December 1987, they agreed to dismantle intermediate-range nuclear missiles in Europe.

Kennan was pleased, though, rather uncharitably, he gave almost all of the credit to the Russian. "Hundreds of millions of people the world over," he wrote, "electrified by Gorbachev's striking appearance at the Washington summit, have been moved to a new level of hope for real progress, at long last, in the overcoming of the nuclear nightmare." And ten months after the Supreme Soviet dissolved the USSR on December 26, 1991, he scoffed at the idea, advanced by admirers of presidents Reagan and George H. W. Bush, that any American administration possessed the power to exert a decisive influence on the course of a great political upheaval occurring in another country. That was in keeping with his oft-stated and historically correct view that one country can never determine internal events in another. In 1996, he still praised Gorbachev for ending the Cold War, but conceded that Reagan had also played a part in breaking the log jam.

Although there were many deeper reasons, reaching back to the Bolshevik seizure of power, for the sudden collapse of the Soviet Union, Kennan identified the basic immediate cause as the demands for greater autonomy or independence on the part of non-Russian nations—the Baltic republics, Azerbaijan, Georgia, Tajikistan, Uzbekistan, Chechnya, and Moldova. He believed it would have been better had some intermediate stage between total dependence and unlimited independence been recognized and that some sort of confederation had been formed, but he conceded that what was desirable in internal and external affairs was not always practicable.

Kennan was equally unhappy about the view, widely disseminated by the Western press, that postcommunist Russia posed a military threat. Seven decades of communist power had inflicted massive and appalling injuries—social, economic, genetic, and moral—on Russian society. Moreover, the Russians were having to create a new political, social, and economic system for which the country's history offered no models or guidelines. They were therefore in no position to involve their country in military adventures of an imperialistic kind. They had no intention of reclaiming any of the fifteen independent states that emerged as a result of the collapse of the USSR.

That included Ukraine, although Kennan pointed out that the relationship between that newly independent country and Russia was "a heavily burdened one." Within the former's borders lived millions of people who were Russian in speech, tradition, and character; in Crimea, for example, the ethnic composition was overwhelmingly Russian. Moreover, the peninsula contained the former Soviet naval base at Sevastopol. Kennan did not at first suspect that relations would reach a critical stage when NATO formulated plans to admit Ukraine to its membership.

The trouble began when NATO, an entangling military alliance ("an armed attack against one [NATO nation] is to be considered an armed attack on all"), began to discuss expansion toward the east. In February 1990, Secretary of State James Baker had met with Gorbachev and Soviet foreign minister Eduard Shevardnadze to make the case for admitting a reunified Germany to NATO. He pledged that if the United States maintained a presence in a Germany that was a part of NATO, NATO would not expand "one inch to the east." The administration of President Bill Clinton, however, thought otherwise and in the early 1990s began pushing for NATO expansion.

Kennan was greatly alarmed. Since the founding of NATO he had argued that the United States should not encourage adherence to it of any country not properly a part of the North Atlantic area. That was because he wanted to avoid anything that could appear to the Russian leaders to be an aggressive encirclement of their country. He fired off a comment to the *New York Times.*

"In late 1996," he began, "the impression was allowed, or caused, to become prevalent that it had been somehow and somewhere decided to expand NATO up to Russia's borders." It was not his view alone, he was certain, that such an expansion "would be the most fateful error of American policy in the entire post–Cold War era." The Russians could not but regard such a move as adversely affecting their security interests; they would then have little confidence in future guarantees emanating from the West. This was a deeply personal matter for Kennan, witness his diary entry of

January 28, 1997: "In the insistence on doing this senseless thing [expanding NATO] I saw the final failure of the effort to which I have given so large a portion of my life: the effort to find a reasonable area of understanding and sympathy between the great Russian people and our own."

Kennan's warning was ignored. In 1999, NATO admitted Poland, Hungary, and the Czech Republic to membership; in 2004, Bulgaria, Romania, Slovakia, Slovenia, Estonia, Latvia, and Lithuania gained admission. In 2009, after Kennan's death, Albania and Croatia joined; in 2017, Montenegro. Even more threatening, as far as the Russians were concerned, was part of the final declaration of the April 2008 NATO summit, according to which "NATO welcomes Ukraine's and Georgia's Euro Atlantic aspirations for membership in NATO. We agreed today that these countries will become members of NATO." Not surprisingly, Russian president Vladimir Putin maintained that admitting those two countries would represent a direct threat to Russia.

So did the parallel expansion eastward of the European Union (EU). Austria, Finland, and Sweden joined the organization in 1995, followed in 2004 by the Czech Republic, Estonia, Hungary, Latvia, Lithuania, Poland, Slovakia, Cyprus, and Malta. Bulgaria and Romania joined in 2007, Croatia in 2013. The West was moving into the Russian area of the world and threatening its most important strategic interests.

Although he did not live to see it, Kennan would have been angered when, on September 1, 2017, the Ukraine–European Union Association Agreement took effect. It established political and economic relationships as a first step toward Ukraine's membership in the EU. Russian objections were ignored, as they were in 2002, when President George W. Bush withdrew the United States from the Anti-Ballistic Missile Treaty, signed by the United States and the Soviet Union in 1972 and maintained in effect by Russia and three successor states.

Kennan's engagement with Eastern Europe had primarily to do with Soviet occupation of the region in the final days of World War II, but it began when the State Department assigned him to Prague in 1938. As we have seen, he arrived in the Czechoslovak capital on September 29, the day the Munich Conference opened. During the year of his residence there, he witnessed, but was not surprised by, the country's destruction. He had always regarded its post–World War I creation as ill-considered; to begin with, it was every bit as multiethnic as the Austro-Hungarian monarchy and was therefore in clear violation of the principle of self-determination.

That mattered because there was between the Czechs and the Slovaks no love lost. In the eastern end of the country lived the Rusyns (Ruthenians), who identify themselves as Ukrainians, Russians, or a distinct east Slavic people—it depends on the person with whom one is speaking—and who had lived under Hungarian rule before the Paris Peace Conference assigned them to Czechoslovakia. Kennan believed that Hungary was the more natural home for them. So, for reasons of their own, did the Germans and Italians who, by the First Vienna Award of November 2, 1938, returned to Hungary the Magyar-inhabited districts of Subcarpathian Rus (and Slovakia). On March 15, 1939, the Hungarians seized the rest of the region.

Even worse, the Treaty of Saint-Germain assigned three million ethnic Germans to the Sudetenland (after the Sudetes, or Sudeten, Mountains), the northern, southern, and western districts bordering Bohemia, Moravia, and Czech Silesia. It was that area that the countries convening in Munich—England, France, Italy, and Germany—ceded to Germany on September 30. Hostile as he was to Hitler's aggression, Kennan never regarded Czechoslovakia as the last word in political virtue. "[I was] unable," he wrote in a private paper, "to share that enthusiasm for democracy in Czechoslovakia that seemed almost an obsession to so many Anglo-Saxon liberals." Then too, he remained cautiously optimistic about the Czechs' future because he believed in the ultimate futility of any effort by one people to ride roughshod over the national feelings of another.

In that conviction, he opposed what he characterized as the "romanticism" of hopeless resistance and counseled the admittedly humiliating but "truly heroic [solution] of realism." In his view, the limited collaboration of the beleaguered Czech president Emil Hácha was preferable to suicidal resistance. Hácha acted as though he were following Kennan's advice when, on March 15, 1939, Hitler sent his troops into Bohemia and Moravia and established a protectorate. Rather than call for resistance he submitted to the Führer's will, accepted appointment as president of the protectorate, and issued a declaration stating that, in light of events, he accepted that Germany would decide the fate of the Czech people.

In his last report from Prague, written in October 1940, Kennan declared his lack of sympathy for "irresponsible Czechs [who] find it easy to dream of dramatic liberation and revenge. The more realistic and more responsible leaders are sincere in their efforts to combat this line of thought. . . . They feel that the cornerstone of any long-term Czech policy must be a modus vivendi with the Germans, and that any national gains based not on such a modus vivendi but on the favor of more distant powers are bound eventually to prove illusory." In retrospect, that judgment is open to question, but at the time the memory of Munich and the unbroken string of German military successes argued in Kennan and the nonresisting Czechs' favor.

Of greater importance, however, was the lesson that Kennan later applied to Soviet-occupied Eastern Europe, and indeed elsewhere in the world; any proposed policy of rollback or regime change should be strongly resisted. Far from achieving its aims, such a policy would lead to a further tightening of a tyrannical regime's grip and to an increased danger of war—in the case of the Soviet Union of nuclear war. Better to encourage Eastern European nationalism "to foster a heretical drifting-away process on the part of the satellite states."

The Red Army liberated the countries of Eastern Europe from Nazi tyranny only to impose a Soviet version. Stalin, after promising free elections at the Yalta Conference (February 4–11, 1945), wasted no time in installing a Stalinist regime in Poland. By then Kennan had concluded that the Western Allies should not continue to pretend that the wartime alliance was anything other than it was: a matter of convenience. Soviet territory had been liberated; why should the United States assume any responsibility for the Soviet conquest of non-Soviet territory?

Kennan feared that the American people had been led to believe that a truly democratic outcome was in the offing. In a diary entry of February 4, 1995, he wrote that the Soviet advance into Eastern Europe actually flowed from "(a) the genuine naivety of FDR and certain of those around him; (b) the extent to which our government had succeeded in persuading many Americans that the Stalin regime was composed of well-meaning people, whose wartime aims were not really too different from our own; (c) and most importantly, the incorrigible persistence of our military leaders in refusing to give any attention to political considerations while the war was on."

Stalin waited until 1948 before completing the communist takeover of Czechoslovakia and Hungary and constructing a Soviet Bloc.

As Kennan recognized, there was little the United States could do from a military standpoint without danger of starting World War III. He never, however, believed that the captivity of Eastern Europe was permanent; the national feelings of its peoples could not be suppressed forever. In an effort to foster those feelings, he agreed to enlist in the cultural cold war being waged by the Congress for Cultural Freedom, organized during the summer of 1950 in conjunction with a West Berlin conference of anticommunist intellectuals.

The idea for the conference had originated with Melvin Lasky, then employed by the US military government in Berlin to edit the anticommunist journal *Der Monat*. Officially, the journal would sponsor the congress, while secretly the CIA would provide the needed funds. The congress attracted an impressive group of intellectuals, including Arthur Koestler, Michael Polanyi, and Raymond Aron. Although most Congress members were left-leaning liberals or democratic socialists, some did not answer to either description—Polanyi, Aron, Bertrand de Jouvenel, Eric Voegelin, and Kennan, for example.

Kennan never regretted his association with the congress, even when it became known that the CIA sponsored it. He did regret, however, having supported covert political warfare. It was, he later admitted "the greatest mistake I ever made." The need for secret intelligence, he later came to think, was vastly overrated. Because most information could be found by careful study of legitimate sources, the often lurid games played by spies and counterspies could, without damage to national security, be ended. Methods of deception, he warned in words that could have been written by John le Carré, exact a price, "for they inculcate in their authors, as well as their intended victims, unlimited cynicism, causing them to lose all realistic understanding of the interrelationship, in what they are doing, of ends and means."

Lasky and his colleagues had not chosen West Berlin as the venue for the Congress for Cultural Freedom's founding conference at random. Like most informed people they believed that Germany held the key to Europe's future. It is safe to say, however, that few others felt the kind of sympathy for that country that Kennan did. Although not surprised, he was encouraged when on June 16, 1953, three months after Stalin's death, workers in East Berlin went on strike against the communist government's demand that productivity be increased by 10 percent without a compensatory wage increase. The next day, June 17, rioting spread across hundreds of East German cities and towns. Soviet occupation forces managed to suppress the rioters, but what Kennan had predicted had begun.

Two weeks after the East German uprising, Stalin's successors in Moscow forced Hungary's hated Stalinist leader Mátyás Rákosi to exercise self-criticism and yield the office of prime minister to Imre Nagy, who had privately opposed the frenzied pace of industrialization and the forced collectivization of agriculture. On July 4, 1953, the day after he formed a new government, Nagy announced to parliament a "New Course." His government, he promised, would restore legality, reduce the emphasis on heavy industry, permit the dissolution of collective farms, and close the internment camps.

Because Nagy was as good as his word he unleashed forces that had long been pent up. By 1954 a writers' opposition had formed within the ranks of the Writers' Association. That did not disturb Nagy, but it did alarm the Soviet masters of Hungary. Early in January 1955, Nikita Khrushchev, who was winning the struggle for power in Moscow, summoned Nagy in order to inform him that he was to return authority to Rákosi, who had retained his position as party first secretary.

If Rákosi believed that the era of reform was over for good, he was mistaken; the clock could not be turned back. In February 1956, Khrushchev made his secret and, in the communist world, stunning, anti-Stalinist speech to the Twentieth Congress of the Communist Party of the Soviet Union. Although the text of the speech was not published in Hungary until 1988, copies from the West circulated widely. Aware that an unreconstructed Stalinist like Rákosi posed a threat to regime stability, Moscow forced him to resign. Although the Soviet government replaced him with Ernő Gerő, another Stalinist, the situation in the country had become fluid. The growing numbers of those in opposition to the regime were not appeased and the pace of events quickened.

On October 13 the party reinstated Nagy, prompting renewed calls for his return to power. Nine days later university students planned a public demonstration in support of the freshly minted and more nationalist government of Władysław Gomułka in Poland, a nation for which Hungarians have historically felt a special affinity. At the same time they drew up a list of demands, including the immediate withdrawal of Soviet troops from Hungary. On October 23, the Party Central Committee appointed Nagy prime minister.

Nagy declared his intention to resume the New Course, but by then that reform program was too little and too late. The revolutionaries, most of whom were students and young workers, had begun to dispense summary justice to members of the political police and to press their demand that Soviet forces withdraw not only from Budapest but from the rest of Hungary as well. The revolution had taken on a life of its own, and on October 28, Nagy chose to lead rather than tame what had become a struggle for freedom from foreign and ideological tyranny. On October 30, he disbanded the political police and declared an end to the one-party system.

On the same day, the Soviet government issued a declaration: "The Soviet government has instructed its military command to withdraw Soviet troops from Budapest . . . and is prepared to conduct negotiations . . . concerning the presence of Soviet troops in Hungary." In a diary entry of November 1, a surprised Kennan wrote that "there is nothing I know that would give adequate explanation of the way [the Russians] have behaved and it seems to me there must be something stirring in Moscow which would have caused this extraordinary behavior." He could not have known that on October 31, the Soviet government had reversed its decision concerning withdrawal and prepared to suppress the revolution.

On November 1, Nagy went further after learning that new Soviet divisions were entering the country. He proclaimed Hungary's neutrality and consequent withdrawal from the Warsaw Pact (the Soviet-created mutual-defense organization that numbered seven Eastern European members). There was then no turning back—as Kennan recognized. He told Melvin Lasky in a 1959 conversation that the crucial limit of Soviet patience related less to the extent of internal liberalization in a satellite country than to the degree of its fidelity to bloc security interests. "Had the Nagy régime not moved . . . to denounce the Warsaw Pact," he asked rhetorically, "is it at all certain that the final Soviet intervention would ever have occurred?"

Nagy's decision, however, merely cemented the Soviet Presidium's decision to intervene. Early on November 4, he went on Radio Free Kossuth to announce that Soviet troops had attacked Budapest. "Our troops are in combat; the government is at its post. I notify the people of our country and the entire world of this fact." Despite heroic resistance, Soviet troops suppressed the revolution that very day. Nevertheless, the Hungarian Revolution marked the beginning of the end of Soviet rule not only in Hungary but in all of Eastern Europe.

Four years after Soviet tanks crushed the Hungarian Revolution, Americans chose John F. Kennedy as their president. Soon after assuming office, as we have seen, Kennedy phoned Kennan to offer him appointment as ambassador to Poland or Yugoslavia. The choice of the latter was an easy one for him to make. There the communist leader was Josip Broz—revolutionary name Tito—the former commander of the World War II partisans who fought the Nazis and ultimately liberated the country without having to rely on the Red Army. In part for that reason, Tito manifested a strong streak of independence in his relations with Stalin, something that did not sit well with the Soviet *Vozhd* (leader). On June 28, 1948, the Soviet Union expelled Yugoslavia from the Cominform (Communist Information Bureau), a revived version of the Comintern (Communist International).

The dramatic Tito-Stalin split confirmed Kennan's long-held view that the Soviet Union could not forever suppress national feeling in other communist states. In a PPS paper he made that clear:

> A new factor of fundamental and profound significance has been introduced into the world communist movement by the demonstration that the Kremlin can be successfully defied by one of its own minions. By this act, the aura of mystical omnipotence and infallibility which has surrounded the Kremlin power has been broken. The possibility of defection from Moscow, which has heretofore been unthinkable for foreign communist leaders, will from now on be present in one form or another in the mind of every one of them.

Apparently thinking along the same lines, Stalin looked on Tito as his number one enemy, the role once played by Leon Trotsky; in Eastern European show trials of the late 1940s, the accused were almost always labeled "Titoists." For his part, Tito refused to give

ground. With that in mind, Kennan, his wife, and their two young-
est children set out for Europe aboard an ocean liner ("the civilized
means" of travel, he called it); they arrived in Belgrade in early
May 1961. By then, Tito had moderated his dictatorship and Kennan did not feel, as he had in the USSR, harassed or restricted in
any way. Quite the contrary—he moved about the country without
hindrance.

That being said, Tito hoped, after Stalin's death, to win forgive-
ness and approval in Moscow without sacrificing his independence. Unfortunately for Kennan, the Yugoslav dictator achieved
a measure of success in December 1962, when he traveled to Moscow to address the Supreme Soviet. Added to that, he began to
issue pro-Soviet statements that made it difficult for Kennan to
oppose anti-Yugoslav attitudes in the United State—even though
Yugoslavia was not a member of the Warsaw Pact, permitted travel
in and out of the country, did not ban foreign broadcasts, newspapers, or magazines, and allowed the United States Information
Service to operate libraries and reading rooms in its larger cities.
More important, Tito's conduct of relations with the United States
remained proper and constructive; Kennan held him in high
regard.

Members of Congress were either unaware of that fact or refused to take it into account. Ignorant of Eastern European affairs
as many of them were, they viewed Yugoslavia as just another
communist country and opposed trade because they confused it
with aid. With their eyes fixed on domestic politics, they seemed
determined above all else to establish their credentials as staunch
anticommunists. But there was more to it than that. Those whose
constituencies included significant numbers of Croatian immigrants felt compelled to adopt a particularly hostile stance toward
Yugoslavia. The American Croatians viewed Tito's government as

a continuation of the interwar Kingdom of Yugoslavia that was ruled by the Serbian dynasty they hated—despite the fact that Tito was of Croatian-Slovenian, not Serbian, descent.

Kennan was apoplectic when word reached him that Congress planned to bar the extension of any aid to Yugoslavia, even though virtually all aid had already come to an end. It is true, as he noted in his memoirs, that he opposed all foreign aid, not least because those on whom it is bestowed came to take it for granted. But as long as foreign aid programs continued, he thought it unwise to leave Yugoslavia entirely dependent on Moscow for assistance. Even worse in his view, members of Congress intended to deny Yugoslavia most-favored-nation status. Against such steps Kennan protested vigorously. What was the point, he asked, of destroying reasonably good relations and driving Belgrade back into the arms of the USSR?

No one offered a satisfactory answer to that question. In its wisdom, Congress did pass a bill refusing Yugoslavia most-favored-nation treatment; much to Kennan's disappointment, President Kennedy signed the bill into law. When that happened, he knew that his usefulness was at an end. The Yugoslavs might respect him personally but they could not fail to recognize that his views carried little weight at home. In his memoirs, he used his lack of success to point up a lesson. Congress would be better advised to leave the conduct of foreign policy in the hands of those who had been charged with it. External interference that separated the power to shape policy from the power to discuss it with a foreign government could only paralyze the process of diplomacy.

In 1968, Kennan and the world's attention turned to Czechoslovakia, where Alexander Dubček, the first secretary of the Communist Party, had set in motion a sweeping program of reform—the so-called Prague Spring—that he hoped would result in "socialism with a human face." A Slovak, Dubček's rise to power made possible a greater awareness of the impulses of national identity, even among members of a party committed to the proposition that nationality, particularly in socialist countries, possessed no historical relevance. Dubček's predecessor, Antonín Novotný, was a Czech who did not disguise his contempt for Slovaks.

At the Central Committee plenum in October 1967, Dubček, then the first secretary of the Slovak party, delivered a speech calling for Slovak equality in both party and state. It added further impetus to an anti-Novotný groundswell, and on January 5, 1968 Dubček became the first Slovak ever to win election as Czechoslovak first secretary. Slovaks were elated. Revolutionary solidarity had done nothing to weaken their distrust of the Czechs, whom many of them mocked as "Švejks"—a contemptuous reference to the cunning but passive "good soldier" in Jaroslav Husák's celebrated novel. While making clear that Czechoslovakia would remain in the Warsaw Pact, Dubček granted Slovakia autonomy, widened civil liberties, decentralized the economy, and began the process of rehabilitating persons unjustly convicted of political crimes in the late 1940s and early 1950s.

Soviet leader Leonid Brezhnev did not much care about Czech-Slovak feuds, but he considered Czechoslovakia too vital to Soviet military-strategic and political interests to permit anything more than cosmetic change in the system. Moreover, satraps such as Poland's Władysław Gomułka and East Germany's Walter Ulbricht, fearing contagion, began to lobby for armed intervention almost the moment that Dubček took up the reins of power.

That he was in danger escaped the inexplicitly innocent Dubček, who had lived in the USSR at the height of Stalin's purges. On August 17, the Soviet Politburo made the final decision to proceed with

Operation Danube, the code name for intervention in Czechoslovakia. Shortly before midnight on August 20, 500,000 Warsaw Pact troops entered Czechoslovak territory. Dubček was struck dumb, completely taken aback by the treachery.

So was Kennan, who in an August 21 diary entry wrote that he had issued a public statement to the effect that "it was a colossal mistake, that the Russian leaders would someday come to regret it, that we would all, in government and out, have to take most serious account of its implications." In an Associated Press interview, he went so far as to call for the United States to send 100,000 troops to West Germany. For a brief time, he even entertained the idea that the Soviet Union might be planning an invasion of Western Europe. In his view, Washington was failing to recognize that whereas it was obliged to tolerate such aggression in 1956, it could not accept it in 1968. Kennan soon, however, becalmed himself. He had, after all, always known the character of the Soviet leaders and the Prague Spring, however short lived, served once again to prove that he was right about irrepressible national feeling in Eastern Europe.

In August 1980, the scene of change in Eastern Europe shifted to Poland, where workers at a Gdańsk shipyard, led by Lech Wałęsa, organized the trade union Solidarność (Solidarity). An electrician by trade, Wałęsa possessed remarkable political instincts and negotiating skills; he managed to reach an accord with the government that recognized Solidarity as a free and independent union possessed of the right to strike. By early 1981, Solidarity had increased its membership to ten million and could no longer maintain the fiction that it was merely a labor union.

Poland's Soviet masters were naturally alarmed. Perhaps because they believed that the Poles were more likely than the Czechs to fight, they gave the government of Gen. Wojciech Jaruzelski an opportunity to find a Polish solution to what clearly had become a bloc political problem. On December 13, 1981, primarily in an effort to head off a Soviet invasion, the general imposed martial law, declared Solidarity illegal, and arrested the leaders, including Wałęsa. Not good, but Kennan thought it could have been far worse. He noted that General Jaruzelski had given his assurance that if or when public order was restored, martial law would be lifted and democratic reforms instituted. He was, after all, a Pole, and a return to the old order was unthinkable. And so it turned out to be.

At the time of Jaruzelski's suppression of Solidarity, János Kádár had held power in Hungary for twenty-five years. The Soviets had assigned him the task of restoring order and forming a new government after they crushed the 1956 uprising. He quickly declared that the Nagy government's withdrawal from the Warsaw Pact was null and void and executed or imprisoned as many of the freedom fighters as he could. On June 17, 1958, Hungarians were informed that Nagy had been tried and executed the day before.

The new government did not, however, attempt to revive Stalinism, and in 1961 Kádár coined the slogan "all those who are not against us are with us." An accomplished chess player, he began to make political moves the way he moved pieces on the chess board: thoughtfully and cautiously. With the patience of one who knows that politics, like chess, repays long-term strategy, he moved step by step to dismantle the terror, institute the decentralized and market-oriented New Economic Mechanism (1968), revitalize agriculture, and guarantee a wide latitude for public expression. No single move that Kádár made prompted the Soviets to send in troops. As Kennan put it to an interviewer in 1976, "The 1956 revolution, although ostensibly a failure, actually changed the internal situation materially for the better, so much so that in a curious way

Hungary is leading a substantially independent existence under the Communist dispensation."

From the mid-1960s to the mid-1970s, the Hungarian economy performed relatively well and Kádár remained popular, but the attempt to combine central planning with a market system ultimately failed. Despite a number of attempts to revive a sagging economy, it had become clear by the early 1980s that economic renewal was impossible without abolishing the monolithic political system. Kádár's popularity began to sink, and although he survived the 1985 Party Congress, his era was approaching its end. Kennan went to Budapest the following year in order, as he told his diary, "to see whether certain of these Eastern European countries, largely immune to the forces of decadence and contrived illusion that are coming to dominate the West, [might] not by chance stumble on hopeful approaches of which neither of the superpowers [was] capable."

In May 1988 the party relieved Kádár of his position as general secretary and replaced him with Károly Grósz, who, though not much of a reformer, represented a changing of the guard. He and more radical reformers understood Gorbachev's United Nations speech of December 7 to be a green light. It was obvious, the Soviet leader said on that occasion, that force and the threat of force could not and should not be an instrument of foreign policy. The next year, on June 16, the date that Imre Nagy had been executed, two hundred thousand Hungarians filled Heroes' Square in Budapest; they came for a memorial observance leading to the martyred leader's reburial. Three weeks later, on July 6, János Kádár died, and with him communist Hungary.

In Poland, General Jaruzelski did not attempt a return to Stalinism, but he did rule with a relatively firm hand in a half-hearted effort to make Poles forget Solidarity. It was not long, however, before he concluded that it was too late for that, one sign of which was his decision to allow the Polish pope John Paul II, who was known to sympathize with Solidarity, to visit Poland in June 1983. So large and enthusiastic were the crowds that greeted the pope that Jaruzelski lifted martial law on July 22. He had come around to the view that the government would eventually have to reach some agreement with Solidarity.

In 1987 the pope made a return visit to Poland where he again drew hundreds of thousands to his Masses and sermons. By his words and by granting Wałęsa a private audience, he advanced the joint causes of Solidarity and an independent society further. The following year the government agreed to begin roundtable discussions on February 6, 1989. On April 6 it legalized Solidarity and agreed to elections to the Sejm (parliament). To the shock of almost everyone, Solidarity candidates won all of the 161 contested seats. Jaruzelski remained president and a noncommunist government led by Tadeusz Mazowiecki, a devout Catholic and Solidarity stalwart, assumed power.

Events in Hungary and Poland were only the beginning. On June 27, 1989, Gyula Horn, Hungary's foreign minister, opened the border between his country and Austria, allowing thousands of East Germans to cross from Hungary into Austria and from there to West Germany. On November 9, guards at the Berlin Wall (constructed on August 13, 1961), the symbol of communist rule in Eastern Europe, allowed people to pass through to the West. In one of the ironies of history, November 9 was already a historic day in Germany. On that date in 1918 Prince Maximilian of Baden announced the abdication of Kaiser Wilhelm; in 1923 Hitler staged the Beer Hall Putsch; and in 1938 members of the SA (Storm Troopers) and their civilian accomplices carried out Kristallnacht (the Night of Broken Glass), a nationwide pogrom.

The day after the fall of the Berlin Wall, Todor Zhivkov, general secretary of the Bulgarian Communist Party since 1954, resigned. A week later, there were strikes and protests throughout Czechoslovakia; hundreds of thousands of people gathered every night in Wenceslas Square in the center of Prague, most of them looking with hope to Václav Havel, a philosophic essayist, moralist, playwright, and dissident who had served years in prison.

On November 24, 1989, Havel appeared with Alexander Dubček on the balcony of the Socialist Party publishing house in the middle of Wenceslas Square. The people gathered in the square wished to honor the leader of the Prague Spring for his courageous resistance to the Soviets. On December 9, Gustáv Husák, the Slovak communist who had succeeded Dubček as first secretary in 1969, resigned the office of president. On the following day, Dubček was co-opted as chairman of the national assembly, which unanimously elected Havel president of Czechoslovakia on December 29.

Havel served in that office until 1992, when, after Slovakia went its own way, he became president of the Czech Republic. He continued to write, however, and Kennan reviewed his *Summer Meditations* for the *New York Review of Books*. He praised the Czech leader for his critical attitude toward political parties: "It is not hard to detect in [Havel's remarks] echoes of eighteenth-century Federalist anxieties about 'factionalism' in the emerging American political system." More important, he saluted Havel for facing honestly the damage done to the moral fabric of Czechoslovak society by decades of communist abuse. What followed the removal of communism's heavy hand was, the Czech president wrote, "an enormous and dazzling explosion of every imaginable human vice." A man after his own heart, Havel helped to overcome Kennan's low opinion of the Czechs.

Up through the nonviolent Velvet Revolution in Czechoslovakia, the collapse of communism in Eastern Europe was remarkably free of violence. But then came Romania, where strongman Nicolae Ceauşescu, faced with sudden antigovernment demonstrations, attempted to flee the country, only to be captured and executed along with his hated wife. On December 3, 1989, three weeks before the Ceauşescus met their fate, Kennan commented in his diary on the dramatic events unfolding in Eastern Europe: "I can fairly say that I saw it coming. . . . It was years ago, before Gorbachev came on to the world scene, that I began trying to persuade people that the structure of Soviet authority in Eastern Europe was seriously undermined and would, if challenged, prove unable to stand up against the pressure. But of course I could not see when the disintegration would come, or how suddenly. It is to my mind a pity that it did come so suddenly."

Why a pity? In part because Kennan worried that the newly independent nations might threaten Soviet security interests and thus undermine Gorbachev; in part because instability in Eastern Europe might increase the nuclear danger. Then too he had always harbored reservations concerning the dissidents who were lionized in the West during the waning years of communist rule. Notwithstanding their admirable qualities, he discerned in them "a certain naïveté about politics." As they came to meet the realities of political responsibility they might find "that many of the idealistic moral standards they [had] been inclined to apply to their Communist tormentors [would] not be easy to meet in the everyday realm of democratic government." Most important was the fact that Kennan had always believed that sudden change can disorient a people; he preferred measured, organic change, an intermediary status similar to that which he would favor for the nations soon to break away from the dissolved Soviet Union.

4

The Far and Near East

In "America and the Orient," the third of his Walgreen Lectures, Kennan confessed that he had "no personal familiarity with [the Far East]. I have read no more than a busy person, not an expert on Far Eastern affairs, can contrive to read in the face of other interests and obligations." Nevertheless, policymakers in Washington often had to shape and conduct policy "for areas about which they cannot be expert and learned." As a Russianist-Europeanist by inclination and training, that was certainly true of Kennan, who, aware of his limitations, always focused on the Soviet challenge in the Far East.

When, at the request of Secretary of State Marshall, Kennan created and assumed directorship of the Policy Planning Staff (PPS), he found that the Far East demanded much of his attention. In an effort to obtain guidance when dealing with that part of the world, he turned first to John Van Antwerp MacMurray, a fellow Princetonian and Foreign Service colleague with whom he had briefly served in Riga in 1933. After assignments in Beijing and Tokyo and a stint as chief of the Division for Far Eastern Affairs, MacMurray acted as US minister to China from 1925 to 1929. Having formed a very different opinion of China and Japan than that held by higher-ups in the State Department, he left government for a professorship in international relations at Johns Hopkins University.

In the wake, however, of the Japanese invasion of Manchuria (northeastern China) in 1931, the State Department asked MacMurray to provide an assessment of the situation there. His memorandum, "Developments Affecting American Policy in the Far East" (November 1, 1935), argued that China was primarily responsible for the crisis, having failed to honor commitments made at the 1922 Washington Naval Conference with respect to economic privileges for foreign nations, all of which the Chinese regarded as barbarian enemies. In MacMurray's judgment, Japan had every right to secure its interests in northern China.

The MacMurray memorandum left a deep and lasting impression on Kennan. In his Walgreen Lecture he spoke of MacMurray's "extremely thoughtful and prophetic memorandum," which warned that war with Japan would only play into the hands of Soviet Russia. Not long after delivering his lectures, Kennan penned a personal letter to MacMurray to say that he knew "of no document on record in our government with respect to foreign policy which is more penetrating and thoughtful and prescient than this one. . . . It has done a great deal to clarify my own thinking on Far Eastern problems." Indeed it had. For the rest of his life, Kennan was critical and dismissive of China and insistent that Japan be the cornerstone of US policy in the Far East. Recall, too, that the first George Kennan was a staunch defender of the Japanese—so much so that the Japanese government twice decorated him for his efforts on its behalf.

What MacMurray taught Kennan about the Far East was reinforced by John Paton Davies, Jr., a Moscow (1945–46) and PPS

(1949–50) colleague. Born in China to Baptist missionaries, Davies joined the Foreign Service after graduating from Columbia University in 1931. The State Department posted him to China in 1933 and, after the outbreak of World War II, he acted as a political adviser to Gen. Joseph Stilwell, who served as chief of staff for Chiang Kai-shek, leader of the Kuomintang (Chinese Nationalist Party). In time Stilwell came to believe that Chiang was more concerned with the Communists than with the Japanese; he therefore looked askance at the Nationalists—and so did Davies. Even more so when, as a member of the Dixie Mission (US Army Observation Group) to Chinese Communist Party headquarters at Yenan in northern China, he became convinced that the Communists, not the Nationalists, were China's future. Best to recognize that reality and attempt to drive a wedge between the Chinese and Soviet Communists.

Davies turned out to be right about the subsequent civil war in China between the Nationalists and Communists, but precisely for that reason he ran afoul of the China lobby, and especially of Patrick Hurley, US ambassador to China (1944–45). The latter charged Davies with being a communist sympathizer. A seemingly endless series of investigations produced no evidence of Davies's disloyalty. Nevertheless, in 1954 Senators Joseph McCarthy and Patrick McCarran pressured Secretary of State Dulles to ask for his resignation. When he refused to submit it, Dulles dismissed him from the Foreign Service, claiming that he had demonstrated a lack of judgment, discretion, and reliability.

As a result of the treatment to which Davies was subjected, and of McCarthyism in general, Kennan wrote in his memoirs that he could never quite recapture the faith in the American system of government and in traditional American outlooks that he had once had. That became clear in many ways, not least in his views on Far Eastern affairs, views that derived in large part from what he had learned from MacMurray and Davies. Like the latter, Kennan adopted a highly critical attitude toward Chiang Kai-shek.

After joining the PPS in July 1947, Davies deepened Kennan's hostility to the Chinese Nationalists and helped to persuade him that, unless the United States assumed the primary burden of fighting, they would lose the civil war to the Communists. However unfortunate, Kennan reasoned, such a result would not seriously damage US interests. He spelled out a more important lesson in the PPS paper "United States Policy toward China" (November 24, 1948). "There is no requirement," he wrote, "either in United States diplomatic tradition, or in the general rules which govern intercourse between states, that a government have 'a policy' with respect to internal events in another country." Nonintervention in the affairs of other countries was the standard practice. With Davies's help he persuaded Secretary Marshall to adopt a policy toward the Nationalist regime of minimal aid and gradual disengagement.

Kennan regarded Japan as the key to holding the Soviet Union at bay. That was a judgment based on history. The Japanese, he believed, had had a clear and limited aim in the Russo-Japanese War of 1904–5—to persuade the Russians to restrict their aims in the Far East to limits they could view as compatible with their security. That mattered more, in his estimation, than the fact that Japanese treatment of American POWs during World War II was bestial (40 percent of them died in Japanese camps).

In its long history of conflict with China, too, Japan was almost always the aggressor, starting with the brutal Toyotomi Hideyoshi, a *daimyō* (powerful landholding magnate) who unified Japan and, late in the sixteenth century, twice attempted and twice failed to conquer China by way of Korea. Opinions differ with respect to whether or not the First Sino-Japanese War, 1894–95, constituted a renewal of that effort; Japan's aggression was triggered in part by the assassination by the Chinese of a pro-Japanese Korean leader.

The Second Sino-Japanese War, 1937–45, was, however, indisputably a Japanese attempt to conquer China. What is worse, from December 1937 to January 1938 the Japanese, under the command of Matsui Iwane, attacked Nanjing, the capital of the Republic of China, and massacred an estimated three hundred thousand men, women, and children. The International Military Tribunal for the Far East (1946–48) sentenced Matsui to death by hanging. He is among the war criminals enshrined, amid controversy, in the Yasukuni Shrine for Japanese war dead that was established by Emperor Meiji in 1869, the year after the Meiji Restoration that heralded the modernization of Japan.

As director of the PPS, Kennan argued forcefully for a reverse-course policy in Allied-occupied Japan, away from the demilitarizing and democratizing of the country, with an accompanying de-*zaibatsu*ing process. The *zaibatsu* were industrial and financial conglomerates—the four most prominent being Sumitomo, Mitsui, Mitsubishi, and Yasuda—that exercised control over large areas of a Japanese economy that maintained close connections with the military. Better, Kennan reasoned, to restore Japan's economic stability—just as the Marshall Plan helped to stabilize Europe's economies. The reason was the same as it was in Europe—to prevent Japan from falling under Soviet influence at a time when the Cold War was intensifying. The United States had learned during the savage war in the Pacific what a threat a hostile Japan could pose. On the other hand, a friendly Japan, together with the Philippines, would, Kennan judged, provide necessary security in the Far East.

The reverse-course policy needed the approval of Gen. Douglas MacArthur, the supreme commander for Allied powers (SCAP), who had assumed shogun-like authority in Japan. After some discussion, Secretary Marshall chose Kennan to confer with the general. He left for Tokyo on February 26, 1948, knowing that MacArthur had cited the *zaibatsu* and many other Japanese companies for possessing excessive economic power. The ideological concepts on which such a charge rested, according to Kennan, bore such a close resemblance to Soviet views about the evils of capitalist monopolies that the charge could only have been agreeable to those interested in the communization of Japan.

But Kennan was not only concerned about the damage being done to the Japanese economy. He opposed the purging of people in government and education who were suspected of having harbored militaristic sympathies or having abetted Japanese aggression: "Here SCAP had proceeded on a scale, and with a dogmatic, impersonal vindictiveness, for which there were few examples outside the totalitarian countries themselves." Nor was there any end in sight, because MacArthur had decreed that background checks be run on all new government employees.

It is more than likely that Kennan had in the back of his mind the nuclear bombings of Hiroshima and Nagasaki. On the fiftieth anniversary of that event, he sent a note to Freeman Dyson, the theoretical and mathematical physicist who was a colleague at the Institute for Advanced Study. In it he wrote that the basic question in August 1945 was what was suitable and decent for the United States to be doing. His conclusion was that it would have been better to sound out the Japanese on the possibilities of compromise. He knew that Dyson would lend a sympathetic ear; the British-born scientist had worked with Bomber Command during the war, as a result of which he found himself questioning the morality of the Allied bombing raids.

Kennan's opposition to US policies in postwar Japan was consistent, however, with that which he had earlier expressed concerning postwar policies in Germany. In a memorandum written in 1944, he stated his objections to a "thorough" denazification: "There is no thornier or more thankless task," he wrote, "than that of trying to probe into the political records and motives of masses of individuals in a foreign country. It is impossible to avoid injustices, errors, and resentment. It involves the maintenance of a huge, and necessarily unpopular, investigative apparatus . . . . We will eventually get caught up in a round of denunciation, confusion, and disunity from which none but the Germans would stand to profit."

To continue to punish the Germans and the Japanese could result in their falling within the Soviet sphere of influence. More to the point, as Kennan wrote in his diary on January 30, 1948: "Of all the failures of United States policy in the wake of World War II, history will rate as the most grievous our failure to approach realistically the responsibilities of power over the defeated nations which we ourselves courted by the policy of unconditional surrender." It was with that in mind that he sat down with MacArthur on March 5. The general defended his reforms but was not unreceptive to the idea of reversing the occupation's course. In his report of the meeting, Kennan called for an end to the reforms (he was uninterested in democratization), a revival of the Japanese economy, and the transfer of political control to the Japanese.

On October 9, President Truman approved Kennan's recommendations—to the latter's considerable satisfaction: "I consider my part in bringing about this change to have been, after the Marshall Plan, the most significant constructive contribution I was ever able to make in government. On no other occasion, with that one exception, did I ever make recommendations of such scope and import; and on no other occasion did my recommendations meet with such wide, indeed almost complete, acceptance."

Almost, but not quite, complete. On September 8, 1951, Japan, the United States, and forty-seven other countries—though not the USSR—signed a peace treaty in San Francisco that returned Japan to full sovereignty, effective April 28, 1952. But whereas Kennan had advocated for a complete demilitarization and neutralization of Japan, a bilateral treaty signed simultaneously with the peace treaty allowed the United States to maintain military bases and forces in that freshly sovereign nation. By then, because of the threat of communist subversion, he had rethought the question of demilitarization, but not that of retaining a US military presence. It did not matter, however, because on June 25, 1950, communist North Korea sent some seventy-five thousand soldiers across the Thirty-Eighth Parallel into South Korea.

In 1910, in the aftermath of their victory in the Russo-Japanese War, the Japanese had annexed Korea and established military rule that became increasingly brutal during World War II, when thousands of Korean men and women were forced into uniform and thousands of Korean women forced to serve as "comfort women" for Japanese soldiers. After Japan's surrender in August 1945, Korea was divided at the Thirty-Eighth Parallel into two occupation zones. The Soviet Union controlled the north and the United States controlled the south; there was no agreement about the future of the country.

Negotiations between the two occupying powers failed to produce a unified and independent Korea, and on July 20, 1948, the United Nations supervised elections in the south. Syngman Rhee, a Christian who had earned a PhD from Princeton University in 1910, was elected president of what, on August 15, became the

Republic of Korea. A month later, on September 9, the Soviets presided over the creation of the Democratic People's Republic of Korea and named Kim Il-Sung, who had served in the Red Army during World War II, premier. By then Kennan had already concluded that the Communists were likely to be Korea's future, but in a PPS paper of November 6, 1947, he argued that because the territory was not of decisive strategic importance, the main task of the United States was to extricate itself without too great a loss of prestige.

"Too great a loss of prestige" was precisely why, three years later, Kennan supported a military response to North Korea's invasion of the south. In a memo of August 21 to Secretary of State Dean Acheson he wrote that "it was not tolerable to us that communist control should be extended to South Korea in the way in which this was attempted on June 24, since the psychological radiations from an acquiescence in this development on our part would have been wholly disruptive of our prestige in Asia." In a briefing he had provided to NATO ambassadors in June, however, he had insisted that the United States aimed only to restore the status quo ante; it had no intention of proceeding to the conquest of northern Korea. To do so, he warned, was to invite Chinese or Russian intervention.

The success of the Inchon Landing in September emboldened US-led UN forces to advance beyond the Thirty-Eighth Parallel. During October 17–19 they captured the North Korean capital of Pyongyang and on October 24, MacArthur ordered them north toward the Yalu River, North Korea's border with China. Just as Kennan had warned, Chinese "volunteers" resisted and, after a second ("win the war") UN advance, Chinese armies launched a massive counterattack that forced UN forces into full retreat. Faced with a major military-political disaster, Acheson requested that Kennan return to Washington from his home in Princeton. The day following dinner with the secretary, he delivered a handwritten note:

> Almost everything depends from here on out on the manner in which we Americans bear what is unquestionably a major failure and disaster to our national fortunes. If we accept it with candor, with dignity, with a resolve to absorb its lessons and to make it good by redoubled and determined effort—starting all over again, if necessary, along the pattern of Pearl Harbor—we need lose neither our self-confidence nor our allies nor our power for bargaining, eventually, with the Russians. But if we try to conceal from our own people or from our allies the full measure of our misfortune, or permit ourselves to seek relief in any reactions of bluster or petulance or hysteria, we can easily find this crisis revolving itself into an irreparable deterioration of our world position—and of our confidence in ourselves.

Kennan opposed a total and abrupt withdrawal from Korea, and he won the support of President Truman. By the spring of 1951, the Chinese began to suffer from their extended supply lines and as a result the front stabilized along the middle of the peninsula. Only then did Kennan propose secret negotiations with the Kremlin, which he entered into with Jacob Malik, the Soviet representative to the United Nations, on June 1, 1951. He made it clear to Malik that their discussions would remain purely informal and exploratory and that nothing would be made known publicly of either the fact of their meeting or the tenor of their discussions. On June 23, as a result of their meeting, the Soviet diplomat took to the floor of the UN to propose an armistice between China and North Korea on the one hand and South Korea, the United States, and the United Nations on the other. Formal talks began soon after that and the war settled into one of attrition.

In the second volume of his memoirs, Kennan identified two lessons to be learned from the war in Korea. The first was the danger of allowing national policy to be determined by military considerations alone. The second was the often crucial value of "wholly secret, informal and exploratory contacts even between political and military adversaries, as adjuncts to the overt and formal processes of international diplomacy." That was particularly true of negotiations conducted with the Russians. They preferred private and realistic political undertakings to contractual agreements arrived at in the public eye and aimed, or appearing to aim, at putting the other party in a bad light before world opinion.

On July 27, 1953, US Army Lt. Gen. William K. Harrison, Jr. (for the United Nations Command) and Gen. Nam Il (for the Korean People's Army and the Chinese People's Volunteer Army) signed an armistice agreement in Panmunjom, in the Demilitarized Zone. But the war in Korea, coming so soon after the proclamation of the People's Republic of China on October 1, 1949, led President Truman and his successors to apply Kennan's containment policy to Southeast Asia. Kennan himself, however, never considered that region of the world to be of strategic importance to the United States. Moreover, he was convinced that France's effort to maintain control of Indochina (Vietnam, Laos, Cambodia) in the face of determined opposition on the part of the nationalist-communist Viet Minh, led by Ho Chi Minh, was destined to fail.

In the hope of preventing such an outcome, President Truman provided millions of dollars of aid to the French—to no good purpose. From March 13 to May 7, 1954, the French fought and lost a decisive battle against the Viet Minh at Dien Bien Phu in northwestern Vietnam. By the terms of the Geneva Accords, signed July 21, 1954, France withdrew from North Vietnam and the country was temporarily divided along the Seventeenth Parallel, pending elections scheduled for 1956. The United States, however, refused to sign the accords because of reasonable fears that a fair election would prove impossible in the north. While, therefore, the Viet Minh assumed control of the north, the US-backed Bao Dai (Nguyen Vinh Thuy), former Emperor of Annam (two-thirds of what was to become Vietnam), acted as chief of state in the south.

At the request of Bao Dai, the Roman Catholic Ngo Dinh Diem, returned from exile, assumed office as prime minister, a position from which he ousted the chief of state in a controlled referendum of October 1955, proclaimed the Republic of Vietnam, and made himself president. Diem ruled with a strong hand, not least because he faced resolute opposition from Buddhists—a majority of the population—and the Viet Cong, the military arm of the National Liberation Front. At the same time, he was under increasing pressure from Washington to build an American-style democracy. In 1956, then senator John F. Kennedy insisted that the United States had to "offer the Vietnamese a revolution—a political, economic, and social revolution far superior to anything the Communists can offer." As president, he implemented his idea—the initial attempt at "nation-building."

In the last years of Diem's rule (1961–63), Kennan was serving as ambassador to Yugoslavia and had little time to devote to Vietnam, but he seems to have viewed Diem as a Vietnamese Chiang Kai-shek. In November 1963, military leaders in Vietnam, supported by the CIA, staged a coup d'état that ended with the assassination of the Vietnamese president. As a result, the United States was even more firmly committed to the defense of South Vietnam, now headed by military juntas; the war, in short, became American. One of the primary lessons here, in Kennan's view, was that the United States should not be in the business of assassinating foreign political leaders.

Three weeks after the assassination of President Diem, Lee Harvey Oswald assassinated President Kennedy and Lyndon Johnson acceded to the presidency. Not having been able to give it his undivided attention, Kennan remained uncertain about his country's ever deeper involvement in Vietnam. But when on February 6, 1965, in response to a Viet Cong attack on US Army installations at Pleiku, President Johnson ordered air strikes against North Vietnam, Kennan wrote in his diary: "News of the retaliatory raid in Vietnam. The provocation, admittedly, was great, but this bombing of points in Vietnam is a sort of petulant escapism, and will, I fear, lead to no good results."

One year later, Senator J. William Fulbright, chairman of the Senate Committee on Foreign Relations, invited Kennan to testify at hearings on the war in Vietnam. What he had to say on that occasion, televised live, possessed a relevance that went well beyond the war in progress; it stood as a tutorial on the conduct of a mature foreign policy. Because Vietnam was not a region of importance to the United States, military intervention was unjustified and unwise. That was true even if the Viet Cong should seize control of the country. However regrettable such an eventuality might be, it would not damage US interests in any significant way: "I think it should be our government's aim to liquidate [our] involvement just as soon as this can be done without inordinate damage to our own prestige or to the stability of conditions in that area."

Even if, Kennan continued, complete military victory could be achieved, a highly unlikely prospect, it would be at too great a cost to civilian life. He could find nothing to recommend the Viet Cong, "a band of ruthless fanatics," but he did not think that the United States should attempt to determine political realities in a foreign country. Doing so was not Americans' concern; their first duty was to themselves. In support of those assertions, Kennan cited, once again, the famous speech by John Quincy Adams in which he insisted that the United States did not go abroad in search of monsters to destroy (see chapter 2). "I think," Kennan said at the conclusion of his remarks, "that without knowing it, [Adams] spoke very directly and very pertinently to us here today."

In response to a question from Republican senator John J. Williams of Delaware, who wished to know what he, had he been in power, would have done differently, Kennan replied that more thought should have been given to putting American combat troops in harm's way. Citing a lesson he had learned from his study of the intervention in Russia in 1918, he said that "one should be very, very careful about ever putting American forces ashore into a situation of this sort unless one can see clearly how and at what point one can get them out again, and unless the arrival at that point appears fairly plausible." That, as we shall see, was a lesson that should have been, but was not, learned by subsequent US administrations and foreign policy officials.

At the time of the Fulbright hearings, there were 385,300 American troops in Vietnam; in the following year the number rose to 485,600. Kennan's opposition to the war would only intensify. In a letter of October 17, 1967, to Arthur Schlesinger, Jr., the Albert Schweitzer Professor of the Humanities at the City University of New York Graduate Center, he wrote that "if the non-Communist South Vietnamese . . . were incapable of producing out of their midst a political vitality commensurate with that of the Vietcong, then we should have recognized at the start that this patient was beyond saving, either by us or by any other outside party, and our concern should have been to soften the impact of his demise, not to try to keep him alive by crawling into his skin."

On February 29, 1968, only weeks before the stunning New Hampshire primary that persuaded President Johnson not to seek reelection, Kennan endorsed Eugene McCarthy's presidential candidacy—primarily, but not exclusively, because of the senator's outspoken opposition to the war in Vietnam. Like Kennan, McCarthy called for a more restrained foreign policy, an end to foreign aid, and less reliance on the military when endeavoring to solve international problems. "Less than at any time in the past," Kennan told McCarthy supporters gathered in Newark, "is any favorable outcome [to the war] visible. It is difficult, in fact, to see anything ahead except either an indefinite escalation, very probably culminating in the entrance of the Chinese or the Russians into the struggle against us, or, if the ground continues to give way beneath us as it has showed signs of doing in recent weeks, a frustration and humiliation unique in our national experience."

The month before Kennan spoke on behalf of Senator McCarthy, the North Vietnamese and Viet Cong launched the massive Tet (lunar New Year) Offensive (January 30–September 23, 1968) against thirty South Vietnamese provincial capitals. Achieving total surprise, they seized key targets in Saigon, reaching the grounds of the US embassy. Although stunned, the Americans recovered and ultimately achieved a major victory. The Viet Cong ceased to be an effective force and, from then on, almost all the fighting was done by regular units of the North Vietnamese army.

Primarily due to television coverage of the offensive, however, public support for the war declined sharply. In late August 1968, the Democrats held their national convention in Chicago. They chose as their presidential nominee Hubert Humphrey, like McCarthy, a senator from Minnesota, but one who, because he had served as Johnson's vice president, was unacceptable to the growing number of those who were opposed to the war. "One of the principal lessons of the Korean War," Henry Kissinger observed years later, "ought to have been that protracted, inconclusive wars shatter America's domestic consensus."

Humphrey lost the 1968 election to Richard Nixon, who knew that he had before him the thankless task of having to arrange an exit from the war; he was fortunate to have Kissinger as a national security adviser and negotiator. Still, it was only after the December 1972 bombings of Hanoi that Kissinger and Le Duc Tho signed the Paris Peace Accords on January 23, 1973. The agreement ended US involvement in the war, but it did not end the war. On April 30, 1975, the People's Army of Vietnam and the Viet Cong captured Saigon, the capital of South Vietnam. But as Kennan had testified at the Vietnam hearings, were it not for considerations of prestige, a communist victory, though regrettable (especially for the people of South Vietnam), would not materially alter the United States' strategic standing.

Early in June 1944, at the request of Ambassador Averell Harriman, Kennan left Washington for Moscow, where he was to assume duties as the US embassy's minister-counselor. One of his stopovers on the way to the Soviet Union was in Baghdad, Iraq, whose residents he described as "a population unhygienic in its habits, sorely weakened and debilitated by disease, inclined to all manner of religious bigotry and fanaticism, condemned by the tenets of the most widespread faith to keep a full half of the population—namely, the feminine half—confined and excluded from the productive efforts of society by a system of indefinite house arrest." He thought then, as he thought later, that it was not the responsibility of the United States to improve conditions of life there. Near Eastern problems would have to be solved, if at all, by the peoples of the region.

Kennan made a qualified exception in the case of Israel, the creation of which he believed the United States should have opposed (see chapter 1). His reason, he told a friend in 1956, was fear that the new state would become a permanent ward and military liability: "It has been perfectly clear from the beginning that a Jewish state could be maintained in that area only by force of arms; there was no justification whatsoever for any other hope." Well into the twenty-first century there still is not.

Kennan never had occasion to change his mind. When, he wrote in the late 1970s, the United States lent its support to Israel's establishment in a part of the world the inhabitants of which had never given their assent, it accepted a share of responsibility for the success of the undertaking, at least in its initial stages. That was not, however, a commitment in perpetuity, because no American administration had the right to assume permanent responsibility for the security of a territory not part of the United States and far from its shores.

Nevertheless there remained on the part of the United States, Kennan observed with some resignation, a commitment "of sorts"—namely to do everything possible, short of the dispatch of combat forces, to assure that Israel continued to exist, that its people not be destroyed, enslaved, or driven into the sea by hostile neighbors. As time wore on, however, he became ever more convinced that Israel was fully capable of its own defense. That was one, but only one, reason why, in 2002, he expressed his opposition to President George W. Bush's plans to wage war on Saddam Hussein's Iraq. Insofar as the dictator posed a threat, he told an interviewer, he did so to Israel, a country that, possessed of nuclear weapons, was capable of mounting a devastating retaliatory strike.

Stunned by the September 11, 2001, terrorist attacks on the United States, the president came under the influence of what, for want of a better name, John Mearsheimer and Stephen Walt have called the "Israel lobby," a loose coalition of individuals and organizations for whom US and Israeli interests were identical. Of particular importance to the lobby were neoconservatives who had pushed the United States to attack Iraq well before 9/11. The overthrow of Saddam Hussein, so their thinking went, would begin a process of regional democratization which would, in turn, create an environment friendly to the United States and Israel. Deputy Secretary of Defense Paul Wolfowitz and Under Secretary of State John Bolton, neoconservatives both, persuaded the president that Saddam possessed weapons of mass destruction (WMDs), lent support to al-Qaeda, violated human rights, and was complicit in the 9/11 attacks.

Based on this misinformation and dreaming, and without demonstrating that Saddam's Iraq posed a clear and present danger to the United States, Bush began to speak of "preemptive war." In response, Kennan cautioned that one could never be certain in advance where a war would eventually lead: "I have seen no evidence that we have any realistic plans for dealing with the great state of confusion in Iraqian affairs which would presumably follow even after the successful elimination of the dictator."

Neoconservatives were not inclined to heed Kennan's warning; they waged an unremitting public relations campaign to win support for invading Iraq. On April 3, 2002, they released an open letter to Bush, urging him to accelerate plans for the removal of Saddam Hussein from power and concluding, "Israel's fight against terrorism is our fight. Israel's victory is an important part of our victory. For reasons both moral and strategic, we need to stand with Israel in its fight against terrorism." Among those who signed the letter were neoconservative luminaries such as William Bennett, Midge Decter, Robert Kagan, William Kristol, Joshua

Muravchik, Daniel Pipes (son of Harvard University historian of Russia Richard Pipes), and Norman Podhoretz.

On September 18, 2001, the Authorization of Use of Military Force, a joint resolution of Congress, became law. That was all President Bush needed. In a March 18, 2003 diary entry, Kennan wrote, with sadness: "The launching of the war in Iraq—the first firing in cold blood—is now, the President has told us, only some 36 hours off." As good as his word, Bush ordered the invasion of Iraq, Operation Iraqi Freedom, on March 20, 2003. Lt. Gen. William Odom, who had served as director of the National Security Agency under President Reagan, described the order as "the greatest strategic disaster in our history."

It did not look that way at first. American and coalition forces quickly occupied Baghdad and deposed Saddam Hussein, who was captured and executed. To the apparent surprise of neoconservatives, however, an era of peace and stability did not ensue; violence broke out against occupying forces and between Sunni and Shia Muslims. Perhaps more disturbing, the Americans never found any WMDs. Nor were they able to produce clear evidence of a Saddam–al-Qaeda connection; instead, they opened Iraq's door to terrorism. In September 2010, the United States renamed Operation Iraqi Freedom "Operation New Dawn," in the apparent hope that a new name would create a more promising reality.

By late 2011, when the last US troops left Iraq, it had become clear that the cost of the venture in blood and treasure was staggering—and worse, ongoing. Although the figures are contested, something on the order of 4,500 Americans were killed while 35,000 suffered wounds, most of them serious. The number of Iraqi civilians killed is estimated to be between 134,000 and 182,000.

In an interview granted to the *Sunday Times* in March 2013, Paul Wolfowitz was asked if the dead and injured weighed on his conscience. He acknowledged the seriousness of the decision to go to war but insisted that the threat to the United States was also serious. Like almost every member of the foreign policy elite, he did not think it necessary to answer for the consequences of the policies he promoted. By then he knew that Saddam had nothing to do with the 9/11 attacks. Moreover, he ignored the fact that, as Stephen Walt observed, the war fueled anti-Americanism across the Arab and Islamic world, and Iraq became a magnet for extremists eager to take up arms against the United States.

Walt referred primarily to ISIS (Islamic State of Iraq and Syria), which entered Iraq's western provinces from Syria in 2014; in response, President Barack Obama ordered a new intervention. By the end of 2017, US forces, together with Iraqi security forces, had defeated the terrorist organization, but some 5,000 troops remained in the country. After a US drone strike killed Iranian major general Qasem Soleimani and Iraqi militia leader Abu Mahdi al-Muhandis at Baghdad International Airport on January 3, 2020, the Iraqi parliament voted to ask US forces to leave the country. In response, the State Department announced that it would not honor the request and that US troops would remain in the country indefinitely.

Kennan had hoped that George W. Bush had learned something from his father, President George H. W. Bush's disastrous decision, to send 25,000 American troops on a humanitarian-peacekeeping mission to Somalia on December 9, 1992. At the time, that poor land found itself in the midst of famine, a result of the violent struggle for power being waged among rival warlords, chief of whom was Muhammed Farah Aydid. In a diary entry of that day, Kennan wrote that he regarded the troop landing as a dreadful error: "The dispatch of American armed forces to a seat of operations in a place far from our own shores, and this for what is actually a major police action in another country and in a situation where no defensive American interest is involved—this, obviously, is something that the founding fathers of this country never envisaged or would ever have approved."

Because of chaos in the streets of the capital city of Mogadishu and the want of any national Somali leadership, the mission went badly from the beginning. As a result, Bill Clinton, who had succeeded the elder Bush as president, reduced the number of US troops until by June 1993 only 1,200 remained. The situation in the country became worse when 24 UN troops were killed, apparently by Aydid's militia. On October 3, 1993, US troops launched a determined effort to capture the warlord and his top lieutenants. The operation led to the bloody Battle of Mogadishu, in which two Black Hawk helicopters were shot down and 19 US soldiers killed; several of their bodies were then dragged through the streets. As Kennan had told his diary months before, "The situation we are trying to correct has its roots in the fact that the people of Somalia are wholly unable to govern themselves and that the entire territory is simply without a government."

5

Lessons Not Learned

At the time of Kennan's death, America's foreign policy establishment (a.k.a. "the Blob") consisted of two groups: neoconservatives and liberal internationalists (or interventionists). Neither group has learned anything from him. Both wish to harness American power in an effort to remake the world in the image of the United States. Both, that is, possess a crusader mentality. As the homeland of democracy and human rights, America is, they argue, morally superior to other nations. As the late Charles Krauthammer, a self-proclaimed "neo-internationalist," once wrote: "Power must be in the service of some higher value. And that value is freedom, or more generally the spread of Western political norms: pluralism, human rights, and democracy."

According to Krauthammer and other neoconservatives, America has not merely the right but the duty to impose—by force if necessary—its democratic convictions and ways of living on the world's peoples. For them, sovereignty has no meaning. Stephen Walt put it this way: "Once the United States is committed to spreading its values [and] turning dictatorships into democracies . . . and once it declares itself to be the 'indispensable power' whose leadership is essential for international stability, it will inevitably be drawn toward the use of force whenever other tools fail to achieve these ends."

In the end, so the theory goes, those on whom America showers its favors will express their gratitude because they will have recognized democracy (with human rights) as the only legitimate form of government (others being so many varieties of tyranny). In almost every case, however, the target state has resisted the democratic crusaders; better to be ruled by one's own than by foreigners. In any event, as Kennan observed, "Interventions on moral principle can be formally defensible only if the practices against which they are directed are seriously injurious to [Americans'] interests, rather than just [their] sensibilities." Even if it be conceded that the crusade is a form of imperialism, so be it, according to neoconservatives. The Soviet-born Max Boot did not shrink from publishing an article in the now defunct neoconservative *Weekly Standard* (which promoted and supported the war in Iraq) entitled "The Case for American Empire."

There can be few more explicit statements of democracy as a missionary imperative than George W. Bush's Second Inaugural Address. The policy of the United States, the president declared, is "to seek and support the growth of democratic movements and institutions in every nation and culture, with the ultimate goal of ending tyranny in [the] world." In attempting to explain how he had arrived at his messianic view of US foreign policy, Bush cited *The Case for Democracy* by Natan Sharansky, a former Russian dissident and neoconservative favorite. An Israeli citizen and (at the time) official, Sharansky advocated for a Wilsonian interventionism on the part of the United States, especially in the Near East and against Israel's enemies.

Sharansky did not state his position quite so baldly. Instead he added a new twist to the old argument for a morality-driven foreign policy. In the modern world, he insisted, security was closely linked to the spread of democracy and human rights; in other words, for the United States, morality and the national interest were one and the same. Or as President Bush, who awarded Sharansky the Presidential Medal of Freedom, formulated it, "America's vital interests and our deepest beliefs are now one." On Kennan's showing, such a claim can only lead to dangerous confusions.

Neoconservatives regularly defend their claim by appealing to democratic peace theory, according to which democracies do not wage war against one another; global democracy would thus presumably result in eternal peace. The world, however, has never been made up exclusively of democracies—a situation unlikely ever to change—and attempts to impose democracy on nondemocratic states often, as US history has shown, lead to war. Moreover, as John Mearsheimer pointed out in *The Great Delusion,* as long as one powerful nondemocracy remains, democratic states have to act in accord with balance-of-power logic. One might add that the theory tends, as it must, to focus on periods during which the threat posed by nondemocratic powers—Nazi Germany and Soviet Russia for example—placed other conflicts temporarily on hold.

In matters of foreign policy, liberal internationalism differs little from neoconservatism; its proponents share the neoconservatives' enthusiasm for democratic revolution around the world. Even before the Soviet Union and its Eastern European satellites collapsed, they had begun to distance themselves from "real existing socialism," although they were less embarrassed by the record of communist regimes in power than by their manifest failure. Communism having been exposed as unfit by its inability to survive, liberal internationalists went in search of another revolutionary ideology and soon settled on democracy. For them, democracy does not merely mean universal suffrage; it refers to political-social reconstruction, that is, to social engineering. What little neoconservative opposition there is to that goal remains limited to its most extreme formulation.

In contrast to neoconservatives, however, liberal internationalists seek to align America's foreign policy with goals projected by international institutions such as the United Nations. Whereas neoconservatives believe that the United States must often act unilaterally, liberal internationalists are multilateralists who defer to the will of an imagined—and imaginary—international community. They regard any talk of America's national interest as an affront to global governance and view themselves as citizens not of a country but of the world.

Theirs is an unacknowledged version of Leninism, which, like Wilsonianism, envisions a world transformed. And thus it, too, is interventionist by nature, if highly selective in its targets. As Kennan once observed, "Any regime that chooses to call itself Marxist can be sure that its brutalities and oppression will be forgiven, whereas any regime that does not is stamped as being of the Right, in which case the slightest invasion of the rights and liberties of the individual on its territory at once becomes the object of intense indignation."

One can see this double standard at work in liberal internationalists' (and neoconservatives') demonization of post-Soviet Russia, which draws on a long tradition of Russophobia—of the kind against which President Washington warned in his Farewell Address: "The nation which indulges towards another an habitual hatred, or an habitual fondness, is in some degree a slave. It is a slave to its animosity or to its affection, either of which is sufficient to lead it astray from its duty and its interest." Russophobia dates back to the 1054 split in Christianity between the Roman Catholic (and later Protestant) West and the Orthodox East; it was Western Christianity's opposition to Orthodoxy that gave birth to anti-Russian feeling. That feeling deepened in the 1760s, when French diplomats, working with Ukrainian, Hungarian, and Polish political figures, produced the forged "Testament of Peter I [the Great]," purporting to reveal Russia's plans to conquer most of Europe. As late as the Cold War, President Truman found the document helpful in explaining Stalin. It also inspired Churchill's "Iron Curtain" speech in 1946.

Whenever a conflict breaks out on the Russian periphery, the West holds Russia's alleged messianic designs responsible. Yet as Kennan observed in a post–Soviet era essay, it was wrong to imply wide enthusiasm on the part of the Russian people at large for the occasional imperialism of Russian governments. It was wrong, too, for Western leaders to set Russia's historic leaders in a row, as though they were all cut from the same cloth: Ivan IV (the Terrible), Stalin, Putin. The latter has nothing in common with the first two. As a young man, he served as a KGB intelligence officer in East Germany—rather as George H. W. Bush served as director of Central Intelligence.

Western media figures have done everything within their power to discredit and undermine Putin's authority, the most serious charge leveled against him being that he regularly orders the murder of inconvenient journalists and personal enemies. President Trump backed away from such incendiary and improper accusations, but when asked by an ABC interviewer if he believed Putin to be a killer, his successor Joseph Biden responded, "I do." Kennan would have been dismayed by a president who would make such a charge publicly.

Then there is the charge that Putin conducts an aggressive foreign policy aimed, among other things, at restoring the Soviet, or tsarist, empire. As we have seen, and as Kennan pointed out, NATO is the real aggressor. As for the repeated charge that Russia meddled in the US election of 2016, the historian Mark B. Smith had this to say in *The Russia Anxiety and How History Can Resolve It:* "Lacking concrete evidence for widespread claims of Russian intervention in the election, Russia again became a proxy for evil in the eyes of Trump's opponents, most of the media and the wider American establishment, especially in the intelligence services and the Pentagon. Even to raise a doubt sometimes seemed like treason."

At the same time the meddlesome National Endowment for Democracy (NED) busies itself with support for democracy and human rights activists in some ninety lands, many of which are judged by endowment officials to be insufficiently democratic. Inspired by President Reagan—who in his 1982 speech to the British Parliament proposed "to foster the infrastructure of democracy, the system of a free press, unions, political parties, universities" around the world—democracy crusaders created the NED as a private nonprofit foundation, although it is in fact funded primarily by the US Congress. Carl Gershman, a social democrat, has served as its president since 1984. According to the organization's website, "Democracy belongs to no single nation, but rather it is the birthright of every person in every nation." With that in mind, the NED initiated the World Movement for Democracy, which presupposes the universality of the democratic idea and the inevitability of democratic transition.

On the basis of those deeply held beliefs, the NED claims a mandate—contra Kennan—to interfere in the internal affairs of foreign countries in order to promote democracy, which entails boosting the prospects of pro-Western institutions and politicians inside the target state. It receives unacknowledged support from media outlets such as CNN and the BBC, which made it easier, for example, to mobilize public opinion in favor of destabilizing the government of Hosni Mubarak in Egypt (the Lotus Revolution), overthrowing Serbia's Slobodan Milošević (the Bulldozer Revolution), and backing the so-called color revolutions in Georgia (Rose) and Ukraine (Orange). The latter countries are of strategic importance to Moscow.

For historical and geopolitical reasons, Ukraine is of particular significance to Russia—and thus to an expansionist European Union. At the conclusion of the Orange Revolution (November 22, 2004--January 23, 2005), Viktor Yushchenko, who was sympathetic to the EU, assumed office as president of Ukraine. His support had plummeted by the time of the February 7, 2010, election, which he lost to the pro-Russian Viktor Yanukovych; the election was judged to be free and fair by international observers. In November 2013, Yanukovych rejected a major economic deal he had been negotiating with the EU and chose instead to accept a Russian counteroffer. That decision led to the violent Euromaidan protests and to Yanukovych's overthrow; he was succeeded by Petro Poroshenko, an oligarch whose ultranationalist government was thoroughly pro-Western and anti-Russian.

The US government backed what was in reality a coup. Victoria Nuland, the assistant secretary of state for European and Eurasian affairs, and Senator John McCain (R-AZ) participated in antigovernment demonstrations; Nuland, who is married to Robert Kagan, a self-described "liberal interventionist," handed out pastries to demonstrators in Maidan Square. On March 18, 2014, one month after the coup, Russia incorporated the historically Russian Crimea. Putin thus reversed the February 19, 1954, decision of the Presidium of the Supreme Soviet of the USSR, which transferred Crimea from the Russian Soviet Federative Socialist Republic to the Ukrainian SSR. An orchestrated campaign of media coverage produced outrage in the West. It did so primarily by its choice of words. "Russia annexes Crimea" suggests something different than "Crimeans choose to return to the Russian motherland." The West did not recognize the result of the Crimean status referendum, although about 60 percent of those living in Crimea were ethnic Russians who clearly preferred to become part of Russia.

Putin could, and did, cite as a precedent the US-EU recognition of Kosovo's independence from Serbia, formerly a republic in the federation of Yugoslavia, in 2008. This came after the United States pushed a NATO intervention in the civil war between Serbia and the so-called Kosovo Liberation Army (once considered a terrorist organization) composed of ethnic Albanians. Although the latter formed a majority of the population, Kosovo is hallowed ground to the Serbs because it was there, in 1389, that they fought and lost a battle against the Turks, the beginning of centuries of Ottoman domination. In 1999, the United States, having chosen to side with the Kosovo Liberation Army, led a seventy-eight-day air war against Serbia that was described as humanitarian in its aim.

Neoconservatives and liberal internationalists have been particularly active in promoting wars and interventions in the greater Near East—against Kennan's better judgment. In the wake of the 9/11 attacks, President George W. Bush ordered the invasion of Afghanistan in an effort to drive the Taliban, a Sunni Islamic fundamentalist movement and military organization, from power in order to deny al-Qaeda a safe base of operations and to create a workable democracy. Despite initial military successes, what followed was a quagmire and the longest war in US history. In a November 21, 2001, diary entry, Kennan expressed his fears: "Regarding the war in Afghanistan I find myself more of an isolationist than ever, reflecting that we, as soon as we can detach ourselves from that imbroglio, should concentrate our efforts on developing at home alternatives to the importation of Middle Eastern, and especially Saudi Arabian, oil—this, in place of further efforts to play a role in that particular region."

Members of the neoconservative—liberal internationalist foreign policy establishment, along with military leaders, dismissed such concerns, even as the war dragged on and on. After assuming command of the International Security Assistance Force and US Forces–Afghanistan in 2009, Gen. Stanley McChrystal told a congressional committee that "the next eighteen months will likely be decisive and ultimately enable success." Soon after he offered that (as we now know) wildly optimistic assessment, he assured ABC News that "we had turned the tide." As time was to show, however, he was unable to reverse the ruinous course of the war.

Nevertheless, neither McChrystal nor David Petraeus nor any other US commander advised civilian officials to end a war that could not be won. On the contrary, they advocated a continuation of the war while offering assurances that victory was achievable provided the United States did not withdraw prematurely. They would have done better to heed Kennan's words at the Vietnam hearings: "I would submit that there is more respect to be won in the opinion of this world by a resolute and courageous liquidation of unsound positions than by the most stubborn pursuit of extravagant or unpromising objectives."

As if the United States were not busy enough in Afghanistan and Iraq, it played a leading role in what the US government claimed was a humanitarian bombardment of Libya in March 2011. At the time, a civil war raged between Col. Muammar Gaddafi's government and assorted rebel factions. The struggle for power was violent and destructive, but it posed no threat to fundamental US interests. In this context President Obama announced yet another Wilsonian project. "There will be times," he declared, "when our safety is not directly threatened but our interests and our values are." On the pretext that the dictator was about to engage in the mass murder of his opponents, the United States and other NATO countries launched an air campaign aimed at removing him from power. This despite the fact that in December 2003 he had abandoned his weapons of mass destruction programs in exchange for a pledge from the United States not to overthrow him. In his memoirs, former secretary of defense Leon Panetta made a confession: "I said what everyone in Washington knew but we couldn't officially acknowledge: that our goal in Libya was regime change."

In August 2011, Tripoli fell to the forces of the National Transitional Council (NTC) and Gaddafi fled to Sirte, near his birthplace. On October 20, as NTC forces were closing in, he fled with his son and supporters in a convoy of seventy-five vehicles. Spotted from the air, many of these trucks and cars were destroyed or immobilized by NATO aircraft. Gaddafi went into hiding, but he was soon discovered and brutally murdered by a mob—a lesson to other dictators that it would be prudent to maintain their weapons and to develop new ones.

On September 11–12, 2012, the anniversary of the terrorist attacks on US soil, heavily armed men belonging to the Islamic organization Ansar al-Sharia attacked the US diplomatic compound and CIA annex in Benghazi, resulting in the death of Ambassador J. Christopher Stevens and three others. After that, the country descended into chaos and civil war between the UN-recognized Government of National Accord (Tripoli) and the Libyan National Army (Benghazi), against a background of a slave trade of captured black Africans. None of this would have happened had

Kennan's strictures against interventions in that part of the world guided US actions.

At the same time that the United States was toppling the Gaddafi regime in Libya, protests broke out in Syria against President Bashar al-Assad, the Shia leader of a secular state. Assad suppressed the protests and a civil war ensued pitting the government against a loose alliance of opposition groups that included the al-Nusra Front (al-Qaeda in Syria) and ISIS. In September 2015, in response to an official request from the Syrian government, Russia intervened militarily, and within weeks Russian air strikes scored significant victories over the rebels. The Western media accused the Russians of war crimes while failing to report anything about the civilian victims of rebel attacks.

The Russian intervention came four years after the Obama administration sided with the jihadist forces and, having forgotten the unhappy consequences of regime change in Iraq and Libya, demanded that Assad relinquish power. In response to his refusal to do so, the Department of Defense and the CIA provided more than $1.5 billion in arms and training to rebel groups euphemistically described as "moderate" (the presence of al-Nusra forces among them was denied or ignored). Were the Assad government to collapse, one of those groups would surely replace it.

In a September 11, 2013, op-ed piece for the *New York Times*, President Putin, a foreign policy realist, warned, almost in Kennan's voice, against a US military strike against Syria. "It is alarming," he wrote, "that military intervention in internal conflicts in foreign countries has become commonplace for the United States. Is it in America's long-term interest? I doubt it."

As president, Donald Trump seemed to agree. Stephen Walt pointed out that Trump "emphasized that the central purpose of US foreign policy should be to advance the American national interest, that the United States should engage with others in ways intended to benefit Americans." It was not long, however, before he found that bucking the foreign policy establishment was more difficult than he had anticipated. On April 7, 2017, therefore, he ordered cruise missile strikes on Syria's Shayrat Airbase, from which, it was alleged by rebel groups and Western governments, the Assad government had launched a chemical attack on the town of Khan Shaykhun.

Assad, the Russian government, and some unpersuaded Americans denied the charge or expressed skepticism—and we now know that they were right to do so. The original conclusion of the Organization for the Prohibition of Chemical Weapons, later altered, was that Assad had not ordered the use of chemical weapons. Putin characterized the alleged attack as a false-flag operation designed to discredit the Assad government. The answer to the question "cui bono?" (who benefits?) was without doubt the opposition to Assad. Assad had nothing to gain and everything to lose from ordering an attack that he had to know would turn world public opinion against him. Nevertheless, the US foreign policy establishment seized on the charge to renew its call for Assad's overthrow.

Because that has not happened, and is unlikely to happen in the near future, neoconservatives and liberal internationalists reset their sights on Iran, which, they insist, is seeking nuclear weapons and represents what they characterize as an existential threat; ruling out war, therefore, constitutes a new Munich, an appeasement similar to Neville Chamberlain's failed attempts to placate Hitler. After the CIA conspired to overthrow the leftist prime minister Mohammad Mosaddegh in 1953, the United States maintained good relations with the Iranian government of Mohammad Reza Shah Pahlavi—until the 1979 revolution, during which the Muslim student followers of the Imam's line stormed the American embassy in Tehran and took hostage fifty-two American diplomats and citizens. Kennan was furious at the violation of diplomatic immunity and, for that reason, argued for war against the newly created Islamic Republic led by Ayatollah Ruhollah Khomeini.

Iran released the prisoners on January 20, 1981, the day that Ronald Reagan took the oath of office as president of the United States. As a result, Kennan wondered in a 1998 diary entry "why [can we not] regard . . . Iran as one more country which we would regard as neither friend or foe, with whom we are prepared to deal on a day-to-day basis . . . keeping to ourselves our views about its domestic political institutions and practices, and interesting ourselves only in those aspects of its official behavior which touched our interests—maintaining, in other words, a relationship with it of mutual respect and courtesy, but distant."

The neoconservatives did not, at the time, have access to Kennan's diaries, but it would not have mattered if they had. In the wake of the early military successes in Iraq, they renewed Kennan's short-lived call for war against Iran. In an April 4, 2003, piece for *National Review*, Michael Ledeen wrote that "there is no more time for diplomatic 'solutions.' We will have to deal with the terror masters, here and now." One month later, the neoconservative American Enterprise Institute cosponsored an all-day conference: "The Future of Iran: Mullahcracy, Democracy, and the War on Terror." The principal question to be considered was "What steps can the United States take to promote democratization and regime change in Iran?" The answer was that the United States had to do more to bring down the Islamic Republic and, in its place, install a democratic government.

President Bush was willing to oblige, witness the State of the Union address of January 29, 2002, in which he used the term *axis of evil* to describe Iraq, North Korea, and Iran, the implication being that those states were similar in kind to the Axis powers Germany, Italy, and Japan—declawed only by World War II. The controversial expression was the brainchild of neoconservative speechwriter David Frum. Not the least reason for Bush's inclusion of Iran in his list of outlaw regimes was the danger it posed to Israel. In a March 20, 2006, speech that he delivered in Cleveland, he said that "the threat from Iran is, of course, their stated objective to destroy our strong ally Israel. That's a threat, a serious threat. . . . I made it clear, I'll make it clear again, that we will use military might to protect our ally, Israel." Pleasing words, those, to neoconservative columnist Bret Stephens (formerly of the *Wall Street Journal* and now of the *New York Times*), who in 2010 justified preventive war by describing Iran—by way of threat inflation—as a "martyrdom-obsessed, non-Western culture with global ambitions."

In a similar vein, neoconservatives insist that anti-Americanism in the greater Near East results not from any opposition to US policies but from a deep-seated hatred of what America stands for—its *values*. In the aftermath of the 9/11 attacks, President Bush explained that the terrorists "hate our freedoms." In doing so, he betrayed his misunderstanding of the way in which other peoples and states view the world—through the lenses of their interests.

Apparently, the sole acceptable alternative to war with Iran is regime change in Tehran, and to that end Presidents Clinton, George W. Bush, Obama, and Trump all imposed sanctions on Iran, backed its regional opponents, and authorized covert actions against it. Some apparent diplomatic progress was made in 2015, when the Joint Comprehensive Plan for Action (a nuclear deal) was signed by Iran on one side and by the EU and the permanent members of the UN Security Council on the other.

In 2018, however, President Trump withdrew the United States from the pact, and in August 2020, appointed the neoconservative Elliott Abrams envoy to Iran (there is no US ambassador). Not to be outdone, President Biden in June 2021 ordered air strikes on facilities used by Iran-backed militia groups in the Iraq-Syria border region. It remains, however, far from clear that Iran represents a threat to the United States.

Failing to learn Kennan's lessons, the neoconservatives and liberal internationalists drove the United States into unwinnable and unnecessary wars in Iraq, Afghanistan, and Syria, wars that have not led to peace and stability in the region. On the contrary they have led to endless violence and seemingly permanent instability. And at what cost? Estimates vary, but according to one report of 2019, the cost in treasure has been $6.4 trillion, while the cost in blood has reached 801,000 (including 335,000 civilians). And there are higher numbers to come, not only because fighting in the greater Near East continues but because of the cost of veterans' care and interest on war loans.

What has the nation gained for these costs? Not one of the war-torn countries has become a democracy, and not one is likely to—social engineering and nation building have failed. Political upheaval and unrest are widespread. The removal of Saddam Hussein eliminated Iran's principal regional rival and enhanced its position in the Persian Gulf; it also strengthened its resolve to acquire a nuclear deterrent. Virtually everywhere in the Near East the United States is viewed as an aggressor, not as a liberator. As Kennan often pointed out, states resist foreign interference in their domestic affairs—and under present circumstances that resistance often assumes the form of terrorism.

All of this could have been avoided if the US foreign policy elite had been able to read, and to take seriously, Kennan's

October 31, 1955, letter to John Lukacs: "I would like to see this country learn to mind its own business, to adopt toward others policies similar to those of the Swiss, to recognize the uniqueness of its national experience and the irrelevance of many of its practices for the problems of others, to address itself to the ordering and sanification of its own life—to find, in other words, its own soul, and to cultivate, with dignity and humility, the art of self-improvement, asking of others only respect, not love or understanding."

As we have seen from his histories, Kennan believed that a foreign policy of the kind he advocated should always be conducted through regular channels of private communication between trained and experienced diplomats. He was therefore highly critical of the practice of summit diplomacy—the effort to transact important diplomatic business by direct meetings between senior statesmen. Because of the sheer number of problems that press on prime ministers or heads of state, they cannot stay with any one of them for very long. Time is precious because other responsibilities require their attention.

Usually untrained in the art of diplomacy, senior statesmen are less able to deal frankly and confidently with the realities of power. In the lectures on Russia and the West that Kennan delivered at Oxford University, he criticized President Roosevelt and his advisers for assuming that something had occurred during World War II to transform foreign statesmen from tough, realistic figures into enlightened men no longer concerned with the competitive political interest of their countries but committed to a new and democratic world order:"[There was an] unwillingness to occupy themselves soberly and respectfully with the phenomenon of political power . . . in the complacent conviction that the common phenomena of strife, suspicion, and rivalry among nations exist only because people have failed to consult the American experience and to listen to the words of benevolent wisdom that flow so easily from the American tongue."

Kennan took particular note of the Casablanca Conference (January 14–24, 1943), the meeting of Roosevelt, Churchill, and General de Gaulle at which the president announced the Allied policy of unconditional surrender. The policy reflected a view of war not as a means of achieving limited objectives but as a struggle to the death between total virtue and total evil, with the result that it had to be fought until the eradication of the enemy's power, no matter how much death and destruction such a policy entailed. Kennan believed that it contributed to the lengthening of the war and consequent death of millions, including Europe's Jews. It meant moreover, that at war's end the Soviet Union would occupy half of Europe.

Unconditional surrender was but one example of an immoderate foreign policy against which Kennan regularly inveighed. His reading of Gibbon had served to reinforce his already settled views of the matter. The principal conquests of the Romans, according to Gibbon, were achieved under the republic, "but it was reserved for Augustus to relinquish the ambitious design of subduing the whole earth, and to introduce a spirit of moderation into the public councils. Inclined to peace by his temper and situation, it was easy for him to discover, that Rome, in her present exalted situation, had much less to hope than to fear from the chance of arms."

What, then, caused the empire to fall from its heights? The barbarian invasions? They simply delivered the coup de grâce. The rise of Christianity to the status of state religion? Yes, according to

Gibbon, although that was only the most important aspect of the more encompassing cause—immoderate greatness that increased with each conquest. Having recounted his melancholy tale of Rome's decline and fall, Gibbon asked if it contained a warning to the present. Might Europe one day suffer a similar fate? He thought not, because the continent had absorbed the lesson of moderation.

Kennan was far less sanguine, but he hoped to pass the Roman lesson along to his own country. In fact, the most important lesson to be learned by the United States, in Kennan's view, was that it was in the national interest to pursue a moderate and restrained foreign policy—one based on a realism that took the world as it is, not as one might wish it to be. Realism ruled out humanitarian, regime-change, or nation-building missions, and certainly utopian efforts to save the world. The Founding Fathers created a republic moderate in its relations with the rest of the world, and it remained one until the Spanish-American War set it on a course to empire.

History being radically contingent, that course was by no means preordained. In his inaugural address, President McKinley had placed himself in the tradition of Washington: "We have cherished the policy of non-interference with the affairs of foreign governments wisely inaugurated by Washington, keeping ourselves free from entanglement, either as allies or foes, content to leave undisturbed with them the settlement of their own domestic concerns. . . . We want no wars of conquest; we must avoid the temptation of territorial aggression."

Kennan's opposition to empire-building was a result not only of his reading of Gibbon but of personal experiences. While stationed in Prague he first reflected on the possibilities for great-power imperialism in the modern world and came to believe in the futility of the effort. The fall of both the Nazi and Soviet empires offered the United States a profound lesson, namely that the attempt to create and maintain an American empire, to subject other peoples to America's imperious will, was doomed to failure. It was time, therefore, to abandon the country's messianic and imperialistic ambitions and to reduce its commitments abroad. The price that had been paid in the pursuit of empire was staggering. Moreover, the projection of a manifest destiny onto the entire world had diverted America from the pressing duty of revivifying its own society.

6

For a Revivified Society

George Kennan said repeatedly, and ever more forcefully, that rather than saving the world, the United States should turn its hand to saving itself. The country into which he had been born had changed in ways that produced in him a profound sadness. In a diary entry written in Bonn, Germany, in 1975, for example, he reported seeing on television the film version of Rodgers and Hammerstein's *South Pacific*. "It seemed like a relic from a civilization separated by centuries from this present age. . . . I found myself suddenly obliged, to my own amazement and amusement, to repress tears. I was, after all, once an American; and if I cannot say, with Oppenheimer: 'Dammit, I happen to love this country,' I can say that I loved, and love in memory, something of what the country once was."

It is true, we know, that Kennan's "better time" stretched back to the eighteenth century. Thus it was no surprise that in 1978, the Ethics and Public Policy Center in Washington, DC, published a collection of papers entitled *Decline of the West? George Kennan and His Critics*. Often he must have thought back to the summer before he reported for duty with the Foreign Service—the year was 1926—when he read Oswald Spengler's *Der Untergang des Abendlandes* (translated as *The Decline of the West*), a book that left an indelible mark on him, as it did on so many other thoughtful people. Thomas Mann thought it the most important book of his era, and Ludwig Wittgenstein recognized that its cultural pessimism held important implications for his own thinking.

Spengler distinguished between a *Kultur* (a civilization in its fullness) and a *Zivilization* (its dying or decadent stage). Each *Kultur*—Spengler identified eight in world history—had a life span of about one thousand years. Western *Kultur*, the beginning of which Spengler placed at around A.D. 1000, would therefore be dead *inwardly* by about 2000. The signs of decline were everywhere to be seen in the nineteenth century, one that Kennan viewed as inferior to that which preceded it. And although the German did not cite Gibbon, he did say that the decline of the West was "analogous" to the decline of Rome; the ancient city provided the key to understanding the future. However much the surface details of that empire's decline might differ from those of the West, the two developments were "entirely similar as regards the inward power driving the great organism towards its end."

Writing in his diary six decades after the first volume of Spengler's book appeared, Kennan judged that the end for Western civilization would come sometime during the years 2000 to 2050—and if those destroying material culture and erasing historical memory in the contemporary West have their way, they will make him a prophet. What was perhaps most striking was his suggestion that "the Chinese, more prudent and less spoiled, no less given to overpopulation but prepared to be more ruthless in the control of its effects, may inherit the ruins."

That Kennan was a cultural pessimist there is no doubt, but he was nevertheless determined to offer his countrymen social/ cultural criticism in the hope of renewing American life. But where to begin? The longest chapter in *Around the Cragged Hill*

was "Foreign Policy, Nonmilitary"; the second longest was "Egalitarianism and Diversity." Not knowing a better place to begin
presentation of some of his views about his country, he selected
an issue that he supposed was "about as controversial as any that
I could find, and move into it as a starter. For want of a better
name, let it be presented as the issue of egalitarianism versus
variety."

Kennan knew that the place to begin any reflection on egalitarianism, America's ruling ideology or secular religion, was Tocqueville's *Democracy in America*. The French aristocrat traveled
to America in the early 1830s, a time when the country was still
the republic founded by the Fathers who, as Kennan reminded
John Lukacs, "did not like the term democratic, viewed it as sig-
nifying a danger rather than a hope, and seldom if ever used it
to describe what they thought they were inaugurating." Nevertheless, Tocqueville discovered that, despite the form of government, there reigned in American society a democratic, by which
he meant an egalitarian, spirit. He did not think well of that
spirit, and neither did Kennan, who felt no less strongly about its
danger. "There can be no question about it," he wrote very late in
life, "the mainstream of American life resented and resisted all
deviations, or even attempted deviations, from its uniformities."
It went so far as to inflict on itself a Civil War "in the name of
union and uniformity."

Tocqueville, however, had concluded, however reluctantly, that
the development of the principle of equality was providential and
hence irreversible, and as it continued its advance it shoved to
the side anything in its path, including freedom, by which Tocqueville meant liberty. Democracies may express approval of liberty, he wrote, "but for equality their passion is ardent, insatiable,
incessant, invincible; they call for equality in freedom; and if they

cannot obtain that, they still call for equality in slavery. They will endure poverty, servitude, barbarism, but they will not endure aristocracy."

Insatiable that passion is, for Tocqueville also called his readers' attention to the curious fact that "when inequality of conditions is the common law of a society, the most marked inequalities do not strike the eye; when everything is nearly on the same level, the slightest are marked enough to hurt it. Hence the desire of equality always becomes more insatiable in proportion as equality is more complete." One need think only of Americans' almost daily discovery of hitherto un-remarked-on inequalities.

Kennan was also struck by Tocqueville's observation that in addition to a stated desire to raise men to a higher level there existed "a depraved taste" for equality, which impels the weak to attempt to lower the powerful to their level. It was with distaste that he recalled that in the Soviet Union the economic misery of the poorer and more backward ranks of the population was significantly moderated by its very equality—by the fact that it was shared by the vast majority of the people around them. The Soviets liked to tell a joke about a peasant who complained that his neighbor had a cow and he did not. "So you also want a cow? No, I want you to take his away." Such ressentiment was foreign to Kennan, who recognized that those who lived well set a tone and standard to which others might aspire. An unapologetic elitist, he argued that elites were indispensable, to be judged by the quality of their character and the degree of their competence.

Kennan deplored the egalitarian notion that no one should live better than anyone else. He could find no justification for believing that those who fell below the mean bore no responsibility whatever for their condition and were therefore entitled to benefits from the state. Nor did he see any reason why those above the mean should be held in ill repute. They were so primarily because economic inequality contributed to an allegedly greater evil—social inequality. As an epigraph for his chapter on egalitarianism, Kennan chose these words from Gibbon: "The distinction of ranks and *persons* is the firmest basis of a mixed and limited government. . . . The perfect equality of men is the point in which the extremes of democracy and despotism are confounded." That is true because equality must be coerced; those above the line will not willingly drop down to it. The more equality that is wanted, therefore, the greater the coercion must be.

According to Thomas Jefferson and other authors of the Declaration of Independence, all men are created equal. That ex cathedra pronouncement was said to be "self-evident." But is it? It was to Lincoln, who in his Gettysburg Address advanced a similar claim: "Fourscore and seven years ago our fathers brought forth on this continent a new nation, conceived in liberty and dedicated to the proposition that all men are created equal." That was the classic statement of the belief that America is a propositional nation, one based not on "the bonds of history and memory, tradition and custom, language and literature, birth and faith, blood and soil," but on an idea—the idea of equality.

Lincoln's words move because they are so well formed. They did not, however, convince Kennan. A great deal of what the newborn child is destined to be, he wrote in *Around the Cragged Hill*, is written into it before its birth. It was simply not true that all were born with similar capacities, inclinations, aptitudes, and traits of character. The evidence would seem to support Kennan because differences in intelligence and talent manifest themselves early on. He believed, he told George Urban, that education should take account of observable differences, that the proper education of the promising few should be more important than the semi-education of the many. To be sure, he thought that those with outstanding abilities should be taught to be aware of their moral responsibility and to conduct themselves accordingly (noblesse oblige). It is important to point out in that regard that those who knew him have testified that Kennan himself treated everyone, no matter what his or her station in life, with respect.

His was one approach to the observable fact that not everyone is created equal; there were others. In a satirical story entitled "It Seemed Like Fiction," Kurt Vonnegut wrote that Americans could achieve perfect equality by forcing persons of superior intelligence to wear mental handicap radios that emitted unsettling noises every twenty seconds to keep them from taking unfair advantage of their brains, persons of superior strength or grace to be burdened with weights, and persons of great beauty to wear masks. In *The Devils* Dostoevsky went even further. The character Shigalyov plans a new social system, the aim of which is perfect equality. Men of the highest ability are either banished or executed. A Cicero will have his tongue cut out, a Copernicus will have his eyes gouged out, a Shakespeare will be stoned—"there you have Shigalyov's doctrine!" There you also have tyranny. As Kennan wrote in a wartime letter to his sister: "Equalitarian principles are the inevitable concomitants of dictatorship. They produced Napoleon as inevitably as they produced Hitler and Stalin."

In 1962, Kennan delivered a lecture in Belgrade ("in Serbian for my sins") entitled "Tocqueville and Custine." There he compared the Marquis de Custine's *La Russie en 1839* with Tocqueville's *Democracy in America*. Custine, he told the Historical-Philosophical Faculty at the university, shared with Tocqueville a horror of an egalitarian society. In 1971, Princeton University Press published Kennan's more extended reflections as *The Marquis de Custine and His Russia in 1839*.

Custine, whose father had been executed during the Revolution- ary Terror, was preoccupied with the decline in the influence of the French aristocracy that had continued even after the Restoration. According to Kennan, "He viewed with fear and distrust the egali- tarian tendencies that seemed to be pervading and overwhelming French society in the age of Louis-Philippe." The son of the self- styled Philippe Égalité, the only aristocrat to vote for the execution of Louis XVI, Louis-Phillippe joined the Jacobin Club in 1790 and served in the Revolutionary army, rising to the rank of lieutenant general. In March 1793, however, after the Revolution had put the king to death, he deserted the Revolutionary cause, and as a result of the July Revolution of 1830 that brought down Charles X, the provisional government placed him on the throne; he agreed to rule as a constitutional monarch.

In his book, Custine—whom Kennan judged to be a man of the eighteenth century—described himself as having little sympathy for constitutional monarchy and having gone to Russia to seek arguments against it; he returned home from Nicholas I's autoc- racy, however, "the partisan of constitutions." Like the first George Kennan, he changed his mind about the tsarist government after having observed it at first hand. So damning was his description that those who view the Soviet regime as a linear descendant often quote him. Nevertheless, according to Kennan, "his abhorrence of egalitarianism remained firm." And so did Kennan's, even though he found it next to impossible to sever his countrymen's passionate attachment to it.

"There are certain epochs," Tocqueville wrote, "at which the passion [democratic nations] entertain for [equality] swells to the height of fury." Kennan lived long enough to witness America enter such an epoch, witness the library of books clamoring for equality, resolute political efforts to "level the playing field," and insistent popular demands that every last vestige of inequality be removed. Not surprisingly, theorists, as the ideology's interpreters, occupy a position of authority in the egalitarian movement; even when their work is left unread their ideas eventually become widely, if imperfectly, known. Marxism, Kennan observed, "has deeply influenced the thinking of millions of people worldwide, and this in many instances where these people were not even aware of the source of the influence. And the particular feature of Marxism that has had the widest and deepest effect has been the implicit egalitarianism that has lain . . . at the heart of the doctrine."

The current bible of egalitarianism remains the late John Rawls's *A Theory of Justice*, published in 1971; it has sold over 200,000 copies. Rawls assumed, for reasons that remain unclear, that the "original position" of men in the hypothetical—as opposed to historical—state of nature is one of equality. He then identified two principles of justice that, as rational agents, men in the state of nature would choose from "behind a veil of ignorance" concerning their own eventual place in society. In essence, the principles require equal right to basic liberties and a social and economic order in which stubborn inequalities redound to the benefit of those who are in a position of least advantage.

Rawls may have been right about what hypothetical men behind a veil of ignorance would choose, but it does not follow that there exists in them a "tendency to equality," but only that it is always wise to hedge one's bets. On Rawls's showing, injustice "is not a permanent aspect of community life; it is greater or less depending in large part on social institutions, and in particular on whether these are just or unjust." What he meant was that human beings incline naturally toward justice (equality)—that is, toward the good—but are led astray by unjust (inequitable) social orders.

We know that men are capable of both good and evil, but to which, in the absence of moral instruction, the human heart inclines must remain a matter of ultimate conviction. In view of the widespread evil with which history presents us, however, Rawls's optimistic faith in man is, to say no more, injudicious. What is indisputable is that such a faith weakens the sense of human responsibility. Acts of evil come to be viewed as the consequences of forces beyond a person's control; it must follow, then, that punishment is unjustified—precisely what egalitarians claim, as demonstrated by the growing practice of releasing prisoners, including those who have been convicted of violent offenses (or who pleaded guilty to a lesser charge).

Rawls's reluctance to hold people responsible for their actions led him to propound a theory of justice that takes no account of deserts. Few people are greatly saddened to learn that Al Capone suffered from syphilitic dementia and died of cardiac arrest, but they are by news that a child has died of cancer. This is the result of the reasonable conviction that the mobster received his just deserts while the child did not deserve the fatal disease.

Kennan, we know, accepted the venerable theory of justice that consists of giving people what they deserve. At the same time, he wondered, as the philosopher John Kekes has put it, why "we find the same familiar vices—cruelty, greed, selfishness, injustice, prejudice, irrationality, dishonesty, inhumanity—in all societies regardless of their political arrangements?" He did not, that is, believe that what he referred to as man's demonic side could be overcome by even the most drastic human interventions into economic or social relationships; the source of evil lay not in political and social institutions, but in human nature. Because Rawls thought otherwise, his followers soldier on in the knowledge that social orders can and have been revolutionized, by incremental measures in America's case.

Some of those measures are of relatively long standing and are therefore rarely called into question. One of them is universal suffrage, which in theory serves to equalize political power. In practice, however, the socialists are quite right to point out that it means little absent socioeconomic equality; the Amazon worker and Jeff Bezos each have one vote, but no one believes that they possess equal political power or influence.

Kennan's objection was different, however. It was obvious, he observed in 1938, that there were millions of people in this country who hadn't the faintest conception of the rights and wrongs of the questions with which the federal government was faced. It is hard to argue with that if one peruses letters to the editors of newspapers. Nevertheless, the egalitarian victory in the struggle for women's suffrage and the removal of restrictions on black voters was not the end; the battle for the franchise has moved on to sixteen-year-olds, illegal residents, and felons. Meanwhile, across the nation, the requirement that voters present valid IDs has come under attack as a renewed effort to prevent black citizens from exercising their right to vote. While that fear may be manufactured, what is not is that the removal of the requirement invites voter fraud.

The so-called progressive income tax is another, rarely challenged, egalitarian measure. It assesses a larger tax *percentage* on high-income earners than on those with lower incomes. One might think that egalitarians would favor a "flat tax" in accord with which everyone would pay the same percentage of income; the wealthy would still pay more in taxes but the rate would be equal. They do not because one of the key purposes of the progressive income tax is to redistribute wealth. More apparently needs to be done, however, because ending income inequality remains high on the egalitarian list of things to do.

According to Inequality.org, a website of the Institute for Policy Studies, the gap between "the rich" (rarely defined) and everyone else has grown steadily for more than thirty years. This despite the fact that at least ninety-two federal antipoverty programs have spent trillions of (tax) dollars since 1964, when President Johnson declared "war on poverty." The obvious conclusion to draw would seem to be that these programs are a waste of time and money. That is not, however, the conclusion reached by egalitarians, who argue that the United States spends far less than European nations on bridging the gap between rich and poor. At the same time, they never say exactly *how* equal incomes should be or how those with little education and few skills can be made to earn incomes equal to those of educated and skilled workers—other than by compulsion.

Kennan opposed the call for uniformity of income. There are those, he pointed out, who work hard and skimp in order to achieve a comfortable life. Should someone who is improvident, who chooses to work as little as possible and spend his savings at, say, the gaming tables, be assured by government of the same life? Or looked at another way, would the expropriation of those well off—a common egalitarian demand—redound to the advantage of the poor? "By my own observation, and much of it from life in socialist countries" Kennan wrote, "I know of no assumption that has been more widely and totally disproved by actual experience than the assumption that if a few people could be prevented from living well everyone else would live better."

What is it, then, that inclines so many to embrace egalitarianism? Sir James Fitzjames Stephen thought that the appeal might consist of nothing more than an expression of envy on the part of those who have not of those who have. Kennan also viewed the passion for equality as the product of envy and resentment. These base discontents were aroused particularly by the privilege of birth, making it impossible for those who experienced them to appreciate the wisdom of Gibbon, whom Kennan often cited to the effect that "the superior prerogative of birth, when it is sanctioned by time and experience, is the plainest and least invidious of the distinctions between mankind."

But Kennan went well beyond that insight to make the case for privilege even when those advantaged were not particularly worthy. During a visit to Leningrad in the early 1970s, he stood in front of what, during tsarist times, had been the Imperial Yacht Club. His thoughts turned to the meals that had once been served there, the wines tasted, and he wondered

> whether it did not actually add something of color and variety to the city for the people of that day to know that here, in these premises, there was being prepared, even if they didn't eat it, some of the finest food eaten anywhere in northern Europe, that here things were being done elegantly, impressively, to the connoisseur's taste. Is there, in other words, not a certain reassurance, a certain twinge of hope, to be derived from the reflection that someone, at least, in the place you inhabit, even if it is not you, lives well, from the knowledge that to live well is at least theoretically a possibility?

What mattered to Kennan was not whether or not the privileged were deserving, though it would be nice if they were. What mattered was the existence of civilized ways of life that set a tone, an aspiration for society. As he once told an audience of anticommunist intellectuals, "I simply shudder to think of a world in which life is *nowhere* led with grace and distinction, where *no one* has the privilege of privacy and quietude, in which *nowhere* is true excellence cultivated for its own sake." Clearly he assumed that there *were* better and worse ways of living, that the notion that they were only different was false and pernicious, and that the principle of hierarchy was indispensable to the maintenance of civilization.

Opposition to hierarchy was, in Kennan's view, opposition to civilized life. "I am anything but an egalitarian," he told CBS News' Eric Sevareid in 1975. "I am very much opposed to egalitarian tendencies of all sorts in governmental life and in other walks of life. Sometime I've been charged with being an elitist. Well, of course, I am. What do people expect? God forbid that we should be without an elite. Is everything to be done by gray mediocrity?" Men were equal in dignity, but in nothing else; to pretend otherwise was to insult intelligence.

John Rawls did ask rhetorically whether his principles of justice might engender destructive envy; his answer, of course, was "no." He began by arguing that envy was not the same as resentment, which was a justifiable moral feeling if prompted by a conviction that others were better off because of unjust (inequitable) institutions. In fact such a person might even resent being made envious. It seemed not to occur to him that even if there were to be complete economic equality, men would continue to be stung by, among other things, another's better looks, greater gifts, or finer intelligence.

As Tocqueville pointed out in a famous passage in *Democracy in America*, the coercion needed to accomplish the goals of a radical egalitarianism conduces to the centralization of power. "Every central power . . . courts and encourages the principle of equality; for equality singularly facilitates, extends, and secures the influence of a central power." At the same time, the principle imparts to the citizens of a democracy a taste for centralization, because a central power alone can equalize conditions throughout the entire nation. That is why, Kennan pointed out, what once were regarded as proper concerns for state governments have become the objects of strident demands for treatment at the federal level, with the result that Washington assumes ever more control over some of the most intimate details of local and personal life.

Kennan was critical not only of the growth of the federal government, but of the burgeoning US population—both from the standpoint of the environment and of the need for privacy and personal space. In part for that reason, he favored a complete cessation of immigration. Nothing of that sort happened, of course, and in his *New Yorker* interview he expressed his fear that the country was coming apart, partly because of immigration; and he devoted a section of *Around the Cragged Hill* to that controversial subject.

Because, Kennan wrote, America was a nation of immigrants, many Americans assumed that there was no limit either to the number of immigrants or to the diversity of cultures the country could accept. He objected strongly to what he regarded as the reckless importation into the United States of masses of people of wholly different cultural habits, traditions, and outlooks. It was cultural rather than ethnic differences that disturbed him, although the two are not easily separated. Multiethnic societies, if often unstable, can be workable—but only if the newly arrived assimilate to the existing culture, not the other way around. Multicultural societies of unassimilated immigrants are not sustainable, however—and that for a simple reason. When inevitable disagreements arise, there are no commonly accepted fundamental principles to which the parties to the disagreement can appeal. Superior might alone will then decide the issue.

While America was a large country, it could not, in Kennan's judgment, open its borders to all those, many of whom came from a background of poverty, who wished to enter. Poverty, he warned, is sometimes a habit, sometimes an established way of life. The United States, as the more prosperous society, absorbs not only poverty but other cultures—and can be overcome by what it has tried to absorb.

Some might say, he continued, that it is America's duty to share its prosperity, but suppose there are limits to its capacity to absorb. Suppose a welcome-mat policy were to create conditions within the United States no better than those of the places the immigrants left—the same poverty, the same distress. Cheap labor might be attractive to businesses, but a dependence on it could prove fatal to American civilization. Such dependence, "like the weakness of the Romans in allowing themselves to become dependent on the barbarians to fill the ranks of their own armies, can become, if not checked betimes, the beginning of the end."

Kennan thought it nothing short of bewildering that the US government was unable to defend its southwestern border from illegal immigration by large numbers of people armed with nothing more formidable than a strong desire to get across it. Since his death in 2005, it has become increasingly clear that it is less an inability than an unwillingness to enforce border controls; the Biden administration did not bother to pretend that it had any interest in doing so. Although the exact number of illegal residents is unknown, or unrevealed, it is far more than the eleven million posited in 2005 by the Pew Research Center. Twelve years later Pew had roughly the same estimate. Given the all but complete lack of border controls, that estimate cannot be taken seriously. The effect of a massive influx of illegal immigrants, other than the exploitation of labor, has been a flaunting of (and hence a growing disrespect for) the law, increased crime (including terrorism), an overburdening of the medical and educational systems, and the spread of disease.

From the early 1920s to 1965, the United States relied on the National Origins Formula to set quotas that restricted immigration on the basis of existing proportions of the population, and thus to maintain a majority of those who were descended from the peoples of Protestant Northwest Europe. While this formula was certainly discriminatory—it was designed to be—it had the effect of preserving cultural homogeneity. It harkened back to John Jay's Federalist No. 2: "Providence has been pleased to give this one connected country to one united people—a people descended from the same ancestors, speaking the same language, professing the same religion, attached to the same principles of government, very similar in their manners and customs."

America was a "melting pot," in which immigrants—primarily from other areas of Europe—adopted the existing culture. That came to an end in 1965, with the passing of the Immigration and Nationality Act. During the debate on the bill, Senator Edward Kennedy offered reassuring and, as he surely knew, deceptive words: "Our cities will not be flooded with a million immigrants annually. Under the proposed bill, the present level of immigration remains substantially the same. . . . Secondly, the ethnic mix of this country will not be upset. . . . Contrary to the charges in some quarters, this bill will not inundate America with immigrants from any other country or area, or the most populated and deprived nations of Africa and Asia."

That as we now know was either a huge mistake in judgment or an outright lie. In a letter to John Lukacs dated February 23, 1984, Kennan reflected on what was already a dramatic demographic trend. "Today I see the identity of these people [his Scottish forebears] and their contribution to American society being submerged, almost to the point of obliteration, by new and immense waves of immigration of people of wholly different cultural and spiritual traditions. . . . I do not look down on these millions and millions of newcomers. . . . It is only their *differentness*, not any supposed inferiority that I regret." In another letter to Lukacs, written a year later, he expressed the hope that the immigration of the Chinese and Japanese would increase "because they are harder, tougher, more disciplined, more ruthless, and possibly more intelligent, by and large, than we are."

In an effort to deal with the problem of illegal residents, Congress passed and President Reagan signed into law the Immigration Reform and Control Act of 1986. Standing by the Statue of Liberty, the president opined that "the legalization provisions in this act will go far to improve the lives of a class of individuals who now must hide in the shadows, without access to many of the benefits of a free and open society. Very soon many of these men and women will be able to step into the sunlight and, ultimately, if they choose, they may become Americans."

The act was supposed to end illegal immigration forever, but it had the opposite effect. Amnesty only encouraged more to cross the border in the hope that they too would ultimately be granted amnesty. Moreover, few of those who enter the country illegally find it necessary "to hide in the shadows." They can always repair to "sanctuary cities" that obstruct immigration enforcement and shield criminals from Immigration and Customs Enforcement. Or they can avail themselves of all manner of benefits. As of 2019, sixteen states and the District of Columbia offered in-state tuition to illegal immigrants, while California offered government subsidized health benefits.

Even more rewarded are the so-called anchor babies, children of illegal immigrants who are born in the United States. Those children become US citizens at birth and instantly qualify for welfare and other state and local benefit programs. In accord with the 1965 immigration act, the child may sponsor other family members when he or she reaches the age of twenty-one. The legal ground for this provision is the Fourteenth Amendment to the Constitution, ratified in 1868: "All persons, born or naturalized in the United States, and subject to the jurisdiction thereof, are citizens of the Unites States and of the State wherein they reside." The purpose of the amendment was to ensure citizenship for the newly emancipated African Americans, not to invite pregnant women from other countries to enter the United States to deliver their child and thus set in motion a chain migration.

Those immigrants who are in the country legally are able to take advantage of "family reunification" policies that allow them to sponsor non-nuclear family members—who can in turn bring in *their* relatives. The vast majority of all legal immigrants, some two-thirds, enter the country under such an arrangement. Clearly, Kennan's fears concerning immigration were not exaggerated.

In a pivotal section of the "Addictions" chapter in *Around the Cragged Hill*, Kennan took aim at television, which not only presides in most of the nation's living rooms but is backed up by several more in the bedrooms of parents and children. He did not live to witness the dramatic changes in programming since the days when families could watch together without being subjected to vulgar language, agitprop, and social deviance. It was not even the low level of nonoffensive programming that raised his ire; it was the passive nature of the medium. If adults chose to pass their lives in front of the small screen, so be it, but children were not able to make informed choices; they, in Kennan's judgment, should be pushed to devote their time to something more active or more edifying.

Particularly unfortunate, Kennan thought, was the extent to which the screen takes the place of reading—and thinking. Learning to think and speak requires a command of language, which, as Kennan pointed out, is the discipline and structure of thought. As teachers, those at least who are qualified, can testify, few of today's young people can express a thought clearly and coherently. Many of their less-qualified colleagues defend ignorance of Standard English for egalitarian and personal reasons: they themselves are ignorant of grammar and unable to write well. If anything, literacy has declined further since Kennan's efforts to demonstrate, by his own Gibbonesque style, the character of good prose.

With the arrival of the highly addictive "new media"—especially the Internet, the smartphone, and video games—Americans read and think even less. For them, as Kennan observed, the visual image has become all important; it has replaced conceptual thought. It has also dumbed down the language. As the late critic George Steiner, who was trilingual, told an Italian interviewer in 2011, "We are witnessing a progressive demolition of language which is being drowned by the image, especially through the internet." Emails have largely replaced letters, and although they have preserved certain forms of the traditional letter they are usually brief and poorly written. In part that is because they are dashed off and left unedited. The days of the "collected letters" of this or that famous person are over. Can anyone imagine, say, "The Collected Emails of Thomas Mann?"

Text messages are even worse. One of the principal uses of the mobile phone, they are often sent on impulse. Especially popular with the young, they can be written quickly by resorting to phonetic abbreviations and ignoring the rules of grammar. Even more than emails, they eliminate the letter's formalities and rituals of politeness and eschew all subtlety of meaning. In many ways, they resemble the so-called social networks Twitter and Facebook.

In 2017, the former company doubled its one hundred and forty-character limit, but it is still restrictive enough to make intelligent communication all but impossible. Facebook provides more space, but no more than Twitter is it a place where one can expect to encounter good and thoughtful prose; instead, one finds countless examples of narcissism.

"Connected man," as one might call a person addicted to social media, the Internet, email, and text messages, has neither the time nor the inclination to read. Nor does he possess the ability to concentrate that reading requires. Having come of age with the new media, he is unable to sit down quietly with a book; for him the physical existence of a book, its look and feel, has no meaning. In the event that he must read a book, for classes or work, he is likely to do so on an iPad from Apple or a Kindle from Amazon. These can offer displays that resemble the pages of a book, but they are in fact images. And that increases the distractions—time to check my email, to look up a subject mentioned on Wikipedia, to see what my favorite news site is reporting. No time to *think about* what I just read in Dostoevsky or Proust or Kant or Hume.

Reflecting on the evils of television led Kennan to call attention to the extensive domination of almost every kind of public communication by advertisers. Writing in the early 1990s, he had uppermost in mind the two- or three-minute ad, which has the intended effect of shortening "the mark's" attention span and hence his ability to analyze the claims being made. What are in fact non-essentials are made to seem necessities. "Seeing this endless prodding and spending," the learned Jacques Barzun once observed, "thoughtful people inveighed against 'the consumer society'"; Kennan was among them.

The new media have brought new and far more sinister methods of raking in profits. Large corporations now have at their disposal the means to gather enormous amounts of data that can then be sold to other corporations—and to gain ever greater control over the lives of virtually everyone. Anyone who has ever shopped at Amazon, and that seems to be almost everyone, knows that any purchase, or registered interest, leads to proposals of similar products. Google, the most popular search engine in the world, tracks all searches and asks users to register the location of their computers or smartphones, which is then sold to commercial sites that target customers in their area. Through YouTube, Google collects information about its users' viewing habits. Insurance companies harvest data that help them assess the risks of different customers—including their eating habits and sporting activities.

As early as the 1950s, Kennan warned that Americans had been slow to note the dangers that the rapid introduction of new technology could and did bring with it. Many disillusioned Internet pioneers acknowledge that it functions as a universal surveillance system—one that records our every move, every transaction, every utterance, and every email. Thanks to Edward Snowden, we know that the National Security Agency collects communications of American citizens. This is a far more sophisticated version of Jeremy Bentham's Panopticon, which made it possible for a guard in a circular prison to observe every inmate and cell from a central tower.

Just as dangerous are video games that have become more and more violent and more and more realistic. They often simulate scenes in which the player is armed and directly involved, and blur the distinction between fiction and reality. Once they became interactive and could use the Internet, they could be used for role-playing, each player assuming the identity of a character in the game. In that way real people are set against one another; and they are not only youths. Rather than work or look for a job, young adults sit in their parents' basement playing video games. Defenders, as we shall see, argue that this may be all to the good because it keeps them from real-world ill or criminal behavior; like drugs, the games can have a tranquilizing effect. We know by their own testimony, however, that some school murderers were acting out the violence of the games they played.

Since Kennan's death, the number of school shootings has increased and crime, which he identified as one of America's most severe problems, has become far worse—particularly since the "defund the police" movement began. It may be true that some past years witnessed a slight decline in the crime rate, but they did so from a level elevated far above that of the 1950s. The principal reason for the worsening situation is that the likelihood and severity of punishment have declined drastically; in fact the very word *punishment* has lost all meaning. The anti–capital punishment lobby has taught the public to oppose all executions, even of mass or child murderers, while academic and media claims of wrongful convictions have persuaded many that *no one* has been justly incarcerated. Some governors used the fear generated by the coronavirus to release hundreds of prisoners, including some convicted murderers, while at the same time, street mobs attack police officers and rioters loot and vandalize with impunity.

Closely related to the problem of crime is that of drugs, against which Kennan also inveighed. The problem is not limited to illegal substances because many prescription drugs, including opioids, are addictive. Marijuana, though it remains against federal law, is legal in an increasing number of states. Drug use in the United States is widespread and devastating in its effects. Some sixty thousand people die each year of overdoses—in part because of the COVID-19 lockdowns, that number has risen to ninety thousand. According to a Centers for Disease Control and Prevention estimate, the total cost of prescription opioid misuse alone, is $78.5 billion a year—that includes healthcare costs and criminal involvement. Many drug users, especially heroin and methamphetamine addicts, commit crimes in order to support their habit and while they are under the influence.

That financial cost of the drug plague adds to the size of the national debt, the growth of which was the result, in Kennan's view, of a spending addiction. In 2005, the year of his death, the debt stood at $7,932,709,661,723; by May 2021 it had reached $28,141,065,621,215. As a result, the government borrows heavily and the Federal Reserve authorizes the printing of ever more fiat money. Financial experts are not of one mind regarding the danger that these measures pose, but surely some end will eventually be reached—as economist Herb Stein famously observed: "What can't go on forever, won't."

7

Nature and Faith

In a sermon entitled "Why Do I Hope?" that Kennan delivered at the Princeton University Chapel in 1967, he gave as one reason being near to nature, feeling one's self a small part of her. In this he may well have been inspired by a writer whose work he much admired—the Scottish pastor George MacDonald. MacDonald (1824–1905) was a pastor for a time but became famous as a novelist, poet, and fantasy writer who mentored Lewis Carroll, won the plaudits of Mark Twain, and influenced C. S. Lewis and J.R.R. Tolkien, the latter another of Kennan's favorite writers. In one of his "Unspoken Sermons," MacDonald had written that nature existed for her appeals to the heart and the imagination, not for the secrets to be discovered in her and turned to man's use.

We know that in 1953 Kennan chose as his first home a Pennsylvania farm. Eleven years later he told a friend that he would like "to live in an overwhelming agrarian country" where industry was viewed as a "necessary evil." The farmers near him had "many times the self-respect and the spiritual resources of their semi-urban neighbors." With such views, Kennan could only have applauded the Southern Agrarians' essay collection of 1930, *I'll Take My Stand: The South and the Agrarian Tradition*. According to the twelve contributors to that manifesto—among them Donald

Davidson, Allen Tate, John Crowe Ransom, Robert Penn Warren, and Andrew Nelson Lytle—industry and urban life alienated men and women from the land and from one another, cut them off from nature, and taught them that profit was more important than a humane way of life. "A farm is not a place to grow wealthy," Andrew Lytle wrote. "It is a place to grow corn."

Like the farmer/agrarian and writer Wendell Berry, Lytle regarded industrial farming as a great evil. Kennan, who loved his farm and never thought of it as a means by which to enrich himself, often expressed a similar view. "We stand by," he wrote in *Around the Cragged Hill*, "to witness the rapid decline of family farming and the reckless raiding and ruining of some of the finest agricultural soil on the world's surface, partly by the developers and partly by forms of industrial farming that exploit and exhaust its fertility."

In the brief period during which he served as ambassador to the Soviet Union, Kennan regularly took advantage of weekends to visit the dacha of Associated Press correspondent Thomas P. Whitney (one of Solzhenitsyn's translators) and his wife. He loved that rural atmosphere because

> it was a preindustrial life that I was privileged here to observe: a life in which people were doing things with their hands, with animals and with Nature, a life little touched by any form of modernization, a pre–World War I and pre-Revolutionary life, agreeable precisely because it was not a part of, little connected with, in fact disliked and only reluctantly tolerated by, the political establishment of the country in which it existed. How much richer and more satisfying was human existence, after all, when there was not too much of the machine!

Kennan would have approved of what the Pulitzer Prize-winning *New York Times* Moscow bureau chief Serge Schmemann wrote of the Russian countryside—that it was the heart of Russia, the ultimate source of its culture and character. "The countryside figures centrally in much of nineteenth-century Russian literature, whether as a life-giving force at Levin's estate in *Anna Karenina* or a stifling prison in [Chekhov's] *Uncle Vanya*, a writer's canvas in [Ivan] Turgenev's *Hunter's Sketches* or a vehicle for social commentary in [Nikolai] Gogol's *Dead Souls* and [Ivan] Goncharov's *Oblomov*. This tradition was continued into the Soviet era by the so-called village writers, nationalists like [Valentin] Rasputin and [Vasily] Belov who used the devastation of the traditional village as a metaphor for the destruction of Russia."

Kennan's outlook on life and the world was so out of step with that of his contemporaries, that interviewers, once they had exhausted the subject of foreign policy, often pressed him on it. He never retreated. "I can't see the answer to the problems of modern civilization," he told George Urban, "in the framework of our highly urbanized industrial society. . . . We have to get back to a much simpler form of life, a much smaller population, a society in which the agrarian component is far greater again in relation to the urban component." He did reserve some good words for cities of the pre–World War I era—concentrated railroad hubs. It was largely because of the automobile that modern cities had spilled out over the countryside.

Kennan devoted several pages of *Around the Cragged Hill* to a critique of the motor vehicle. While the railway tended to gather people together around an urban terminus, the automobile disintegrated all that the railway had brought together. It was the enemy of the sense of community, not only with reference to residence but to travel. Having to drive—there was no railway line—from Princeton to his farm, Kennan could not recall ever having met another human being.

He was just getting started. An inveterate walker himself, Kennan charged the motor vehicle with being distinctly unhealthy—walking being the most readily accessible form of exercise. The vast majority of children, he pointed out correctly, once walked to and from school. "Today they sit, passive, bored, and inactive, in the family car or the school bus." That the automobile has been a boon to criminals is almost too obvious to mention. Although it is true that driving the automobile can be an addiction, it is by now so much a part of modern life that it is unlikely ever to be replaced. Kennan's proposed solution to the problem was public transportation, but he must have known that it is too late for that. More likely it will be something worse than the traditional automobile—the self-driving vehicle.

In a 1959 interview with Melvin Lasky, then the editor of the distinguished British magazine *Encounter*, Kennan had also raised the subject of industrialism and urbanism. He contrasted the Marxists, who saw the Industrial Revolution only as the exploitation of man by man, with those, like himself, who saw urbanization itself and the things that the machine does to man as the real trouble. He then added that he could not help but think of the tremendous insight buried in one of Chekhov's stories.

In "A Medical Case," a factory owner and widow calls a doctor to her home; her daughter, twenty years of age, is ill. The doctor has never demonstrated any particular interest in factories, but he has had occasions to treat factory owners; and "when he saw some factory in the distance or up close, he thought each time of how quiet and peaceful everything was outside, and how inside there must be the impenetrable ignorance and obtuse egoism of the owners, the tedious, unhealthy labor of the workers, squabbles, vodka, vermin." As he approaches the house, he catches a glimpse of five large buildings with smokestacks and some pathetic little gardens.

A governess greets and leads him to the patient, whom he quickly discovers to be perfectly well.

Nevertheless, the distraught mother pleads with the doctor to stay the night, and he agrees. After dinner, he walks outside and looks out over the surrounding area. "As a physician, he could make correct judgments about chronic ailments the fundamental cause of which was incomprehensible and incurable, and he looked at factories as a misunderstanding, the cause of which was also obscure and irremediable, and while he did not consider all the improvements in the workers' lives superfluous, he saw them as the equivalent of treating an incurable illness."

As Kennan explained to Lasky, the doctor

> arrived at the conclusion that all of this—the workers and their misery and the owners and their plight—was a kind of monstrous "misunderstanding." Think what a much more charitable interpretation that was than the interpretation of Marx. And he was absolutely correct—it is a huge misunderstanding—a misunderstanding of hasty and thoughtless industrialism in which both the entrepreneurs and the workers were all embraced and which we are just now beginning to disentangle, and in a much more profound and much more charitable way, I think, than Marx tried to disentangle it.

In early 1950, only months before North Korea's invasion of South Korea, the State Department sent Kennan on a fact-finding mission to Latin America. He traveled, of course, by train and woke up early on a Sunday morning as St. Louis rolled into view. In his diary, he penned an unsparing account of the vast difference between the farm and the city.

> For cities there is something sinister and pitiless about the dawn. The farm, secure in its humility and its submission, can take it. It can even welcome it, joyously, like the return of an old friend. But

the city, still sleeping, cowers restlessly under it, particularly under the Sabbath dawn. In this chill, calm light, the city is helpless, and in a sense, naked. Its dreams are disturbed, its pretense, its ugliness, its impermanence exposed, its failure documented, its verdict written. The darkness, with its neon signs, its eroticism, and its intoxication, was protective and forgiving—tolerant of dreams and of delusions. The dawn is judgment: merciless and impassive.

St. Louis and other American cities, Kennan wrote in an equally scathing section of *Around the Cragged Hill*, were surrounded by regions of suburbia and exurbia which had the drawbacks of both city and country and the virtues of neither. At the same time, the city centers were "abandoned to such of the Third World elements as can crowd into them, and left to serve as the homes of crime, demoralization, misery, and degradation." That echoes what Spengler wrote in *The Decline of the West:* "In place of a world, there is a *city, a point*, in which the whole life of broad regions is collecting while the rest dries up. In place of a type-true people, born of and grown on the soil, there is a new sort of nomad, cohering unstably in fluid masses, the parasitical city dweller, traditionless, utterly matter-of-fact, religionless, clever, unfruitful, deeply contemptuous of the countryman and especially that highest form of countryman, the country gentleman."

Since 1993, when Kennan penned his words, the situation in American cities has become calamitous. Crime is now so widespread and violent that certain areas are quite literally war zones. The number of homeless, mentally ill, and often drug-addicted people is so great that tent cities have sprung up. There are currently twenty-seven major tent cities in the United States, including Portland, Seattle, Chicago, Oakland, and Los Angeles and with them unsanitary conditions and the spread of disease.

Added to this, in urban areas violent street mobs have burned buildings, looted businesses, vandalized monuments, and attacked police officers with impunity. These mobs closely resemble the anarchic and violent revolutionaries in February (March in the Gregorian calendar) 1917 Russia—described in detail by Aleksandr Solzhenitsyn. "We don't want to live with police anymore," they cried. "We want to live in total freedom." What that meant was that "each inhabitant of the capital, each of its two and a half million, was left to fend for himself: there was no one to guide and protect him. Released criminals and the urban rabble were doing as they pleased." Petrograd spent all evening and night catching and killing its own police. They smashed windows and looted shops. The government did nothing—not a single shot, not a single arrest.

Not having lived long enough to witness the contemporary American assault on civilization, Kennan identified environmental deterioration as the greatest danger confronting urban-industrial societies—only nuclear weapons posed a greater threat to the future of mankind. He was at heart an old-fashioned conservationist who had much in common with Wendell Berry, who posits two ways of approaching nature—as exploiter or as nurturer. The former is a specialist; the latter is not. The standard of the exploiter is efficiency; the standard of the nurturer is care. The goal of the exploiter is money; the goal of the nurturer is health—that of the land, family, community, country, and self.

During the 1950s, however, Kennan's alarm at the harm men were doing to nature began to grow. We know that he read and admired *The Sea Around Us*, Rachel Carson's poetic guide to what was known and what remained mysterious about the oceans. He must have been moved by Carson's loving portrait of the seas, with which he had forged a close bond. Whenever possible, he chose the ocean liner over the airplane—at sea he could be reminded of what civilized travel had once been. Even more important was the pleasure he experienced as he sailed Scandinavian waters at the helm of his *Nagawicka*, a thirty-two-foot Norwegian "motor-sailor." That acquisition, he wrote in an unpublished note of 1970, responded to some deep psychic need; it was a symbol of liberation from mainland life.

In the same year that Kennan drafted that note, *Foreign Affairs* published his "To Prevent a World Wasteland," in which he proposed the creation of an International Environmental Agency composed of scientists and experts who would set aside the interests of their own countries and act only in the interest of mankind. It was not, he assured readers, a matter of giving orders, of telling governments what to do.

Kennan's growing, and legitimate concern over the thoughtless and irresponsible exploitation of nature did throw him into the arms of those for whom environmentalism aimed less at conservation than at reconstructing the social order. The United Nations Environment Programme (founded in 1972) threatens that "with little over 10 years left to meet the target date of 2030, the world will need to pick up the pace and put greater efforts in finding better solutions to pollution, climate change and biodiversity loss in order to truly transform societies and economies."

That is not what Kennan had in mind. International cooperation of the UN kind runs an enormous risk of tyranny, for in the political atmosphere of the contemporary world it is difficult to find environmentalists who have no political agendas. Although he did not live long enough to take the measure of the theory of anthropogenic climate change, he would without doubt have recognized it as a political movement. True scientific theories are never settled, as climate change activists claim; they are always open to challenge. Nor would it have escaped his notice that international bureaucracies take aim primarily at Western nations; non-Western nations almost always are given passes, even when they are clearly guilty of polluting and other sins against the natural world.

What Kennan did have in mind was some form of *dirigisme* (from the French *diriger*, "to direct"). He did not mean that the government should manage any part of the economic process, but rather that it should establish limits beyond which free enterprise would not be permitted to go. When, he explained, it came to pollution from a smokestack, the cutting of a forest, or the disposal of noxious waste products—he would certainly have added the turn to wind turbines that interrupt the landscape, disrupt habitats, and kill birds and bats—it should be up to public authority to set the boundary between the permissible and the impermissible. He was not, then, seeking to remedy "social injustice," but to rectify the injustice that mankind was doing to itself by permitting the machine to become its master rather than its servant, by adopting a rapacious and irresponsible attitude toward nature.

If, Kennan believed, there was any hope of reversing, or at least slowing, the nation's decline, it rested with the young. How then, he asked in a diary entry of August 5, 1956, "can one sit by and see them become older without really maturing . . . to say nothing of the poverty of education, the incoherence of speech, the never-ending mumbling of stereotypes, the pretense of tough, disillusioned taciturnity." He might have added the seemingly inexplicable anger that had seized members of the most pampered segment of the population. Clearly, he was deeply concerned about their future as protests erupted across the nation's campuses in the late sixties. When, in December 1967, he was invited to deliver a brief speech at the dedication of a new library at Swarthmore College, he thought to use the occasion to warn of the dangers of student radicalism.

There was a time, he told his audience, when universities were places of semimonastic withdrawal from participation in contemporary life, the purpose of which was to reflect calmly on life in its more permanent aspects. In modern America, students were anything but monks in search of knowledge, to say nothing of wisdom; they were completely absorbed in the affairs of the passing world. Moreover, these affairs were discussed not after calm consideration but, in the words of W. B. Yeats, with "passionate intensity." Kennan distinguished between angry and violent militants who exhibited an extraordinary degree of certainty concerning their own rectitude and the iniquity of those with whom they disagreed, and those who called for "making love, not war" and believed that drugs would release hitherto unsuspected and untapped human powers. He wondered if the members of either group had any real claim to being considered students.

Why, Kennan asked friends at Princeton and Harvard, could their institutions not create a special college for those who were interested in the humanities and who displayed a serious competence in their field. They would be told that they would be committing themselves to an austere program of study. "We will have no pre-arranged sporting activities. You can go out and take a walk or play tennis, but no football, no baseball, no mass-audiences. This is going to be a place of contemplation. . . . We will not have music played all over the campus, nor are you going to have high-fidelity equipment installed in your rooms. We will exclude television and all the other trivia of communication. . . . You are going to live with books."

There were, to no one's surprise, no takers, but drawing on his greater experience of life and the world, Kennan warned the young, for most of whom history had become "irrelevant," that past attempts "to storm the bastions of society in the name of utopian

beliefs . . . to achieve the elimination of all evil and the realization
of the millennium within their own time" had done far more harm
than humble efforts to bring a little order and civility to one's immediate surroundings. Looking back years later, he told the *New
Yorker* interviewer that "if you're going to change a civilization, it
can be done only as the gardener does it, not as the engineer does
it. That is, it's got to be done in harmony with the rules of nature
and can't all be done overnight."

In his most provocative challenge to the sixties radicals' conven-
tional wisdom, Kennan declared that "the decisive seat of evil in
this world is not in social and political institutions . . . but simply
in the weakness and imperfection of the human soul itself." That
had to be borne in mind when students demanded unrestricted
liberty. "The effect of liberty to individuals," Burke observed, "is
that they may do what they please: We ought to see what it will
please them to do, before we risque congratulations, which may be
soon turned into complaints." Kennan agreed. In his view liberty
was real only to the extent that it placed on itself certain obligations and restraints. In the cultivation of unrestrained, undisci-
plined behavior, he perceived not only a great danger to the fabric
of society but a selfishness, hardheartedness, callousness, and indifference to the feelings of others.

When, on January 21, 1968, the *New York Times Magazine* published Kennan's remarks under the title "Rebels Without a Program," all hell broke loose. Incensed students and their equally
irate defenders deluged editors and Kennan himself with letters of
outrage. As Kennan could not help but notice, many of the young
men complained bitterly of the draft, though few of them mentioned fear or the disruption of their life plans as reasons for their
indignation; it was only, they wished Kennan to believe, their unwillingness to violate their conscience by participating in an unjust

war. The undoubted plight of Black Americans, the real and alleged evils of the military and corporations, and the moral compromises said to have been made by older generations were also
subjected to withering criticism.

Almost everything that Kennan had said came under attack.
"Every fiber of my being," a Notre Dame senior wrote, "every holy
and intimate experience I have known cries out against" the idea
that the source of evil lies within each of us. Improved institutions, a member of Columbia's Students for a Democratic Society
(SDS) insisted, could make "war and poverty, exploitation and
racism" disappear. A female graduate student at Columbia opined
that students would be less likely to take to the streets "if more
social science departments offered courses about race relations,
urban problems, and Vietnam. Many students find that their university experience is divorced from reality and therefore reject the
scholastic tradition which, as Mr. Kennan says, has so much to
offer."

Kennan read every letter he received and made extensive notes.
He was not, however, well pleased to be informed by a recent Dart-
mouth graduate that reforms were not enough: "It will take nothing
less than the radical transformation of the economic, social, and
political structure of this society." A student at the University of
Rochester found the idea of withdrawing to a study "repugnant . . .
we all share in the crime of complacency." A recent Harvard graduate gave it as his opinion that Kennan sometimes sounded like
Hitler and that hippies "have as much chance of discovering truths,
through their search for inner happiness and experience, as schol-
ars do in all of their books and secondhand knowledge." Contrary
to what Kennan had averred, another wrote, "Much of the creative
and constructive thought of our age has been facilitated by drug
experience."

In a long reply to his critics, Kennan wondered out loud what, given their outlook, they were doing on campuses. He knew the answer of course: they were after a credential, a good time, and a means of avoiding the draft. From the student radicals' various frustrations, he concluded that they came almost exclusively from urban areas and, as a result, gave no evidence of having any real interest in nature, much less in protecting and preserving it; student radicalism was, in short, a distinctly urban phenomenon.

That the young radicals were relentless in their pursuit of what they called justice did not impress Kennan. He pointed out that humanity was often said to be divided between those who, in their political philosophy, placed the emphasis on order and those who placed it on justice. The latter, he argued, was always imperfect—and, he might have added, open to differing definitions. The good order of society, on the other hand, was more certain. It encouraged men and women to observe the amenities, to conduct themselves with more decency than is natural. The benefit of the doubt should lie, therefore, with the forces of order.

Kennan also questioned whether it was really the misery of others that troubled the students. Was their outrage at injustices, real and imagined, not the expression of some inner need to which the objects had only an accidental relevance? If the war in Vietnam should end and the draft be eliminated, would these restless youths not remain on the prowl for causes? The question was rhetorical, because Kennan believed that the student radicals were the products "of the sickly secularism of [American] society." Deprived by secularization of any sense of purpose or meaning, they experienced a profound discontent that could be alleviated only by discovering, or creating for themselves, some reason to live. In the vast majority of cases, they looked to sociopolitical utopias.

Having sketched a collective portrait of America's student radical, Kennan drew a parallel with the nineteenth-century Russian Populist student, who was also in search of utopia. In 1868, one hundred years before the "year of revolution" in the United States and the Western world, Pyotr Lavrov began serialized publication of *Historical Letters* in which he argued that intellectuals had first to educate the peasants politically before they could be expected to rise against tsarist oppression. With that in mind, socialist circles began to spring up in university cities across Russia, the most influential being the Tchaikovsky Circle, founded in St. Petersburg in 1869.

Among members of the circle was Sergei Stepnyak-Kravchinsky. He and others answered Lavrov's summons to "go to the people" and help them to understand that they possessed the power to destroy the existing system and establish a new social order. They were to have even less success than the sixties radicals who failed to turn America's blue-collar workers into revolutionaries.

Beginning in the late spring of 1874, some two thousand young men and women poured out of Russian cities to educate the people. They traveled from village to village, alone or in small groups, spreading the socialist gospel. In his memoirs, Kravchinsky recalled their fervor: "It was not yet a political movement. Rather it was like a religious movement, with all the infectious nature of such movements. Men were trying not just to reach a certain practical end, but also to satisfy a deeply felt duty, an aspiration for moral perfection."

Disillusionment was, however, not long in coming. The peasants confronted the student-missionaries at best with incomprehension and suspicion, at worst with open hostility. They remained devoted to the tsar and the Orthodox Church, both of which the students reviled. Instead of developing a revolutionary consciousness, they reported the young to the police, who placed some sixteen hundred of them, including Kravchinsky, under arrest. He, however, managed to escape his captors and reach the Balkans.

Kravchinsky, along with others like him, now decided that the authentic need of the moment was for an organization of small groups of professional revolutionaries who would not shrink from the resort to violence. In 1878 he returned to Russia, where he assassinated General Nikolai Mesentzev, head of the secret police, in the streets of St. Petersburg. He went underground until 1880 when he again escaped into exile, first to Switzerland and then to London, where he established the Society of Friends of Russian Freedom. It was there that the first George Kennan met him and joined his society. In an editorial in *Free Russia*, the society's house organ, Stepnyak, as he was known in England, wrote that "the great stream of sympathy with our cause, spreading now over the whole English-speaking world, has its source in the work of a man whose name will be associated forever with our emancipation, George Kennan."

Perhaps because he had settled in England, Stepnyak had turned to a less violent, a more reformist, socialism, but not all of his former comrades followed suit. Some moved on to Narodnaya Volya ("People's Will," formed in 1879), a terrorist organization responsible for the assassination of Tsar Alexander II (the "Reformist Tsar") in 1881. And as Tibor Szamuely, the Moscow-born historian pointed out, without the experience of Narodnaya Volya, to which Lenin referred again and again, it is hardly possible to imagine the creation of a "party of a new type." Kennan agreed and, in his reply to critics, warned that it was from such radical students, "frustrated in their efforts to help the Russian peasant, that Lenin forged his highly disciplined faction."

Based on the letters Kennan received from critics of his Swarthmore talk, few students accepted his criticisms. Then, only a few months after the *New York Times* published a version of the talk, the nation was shaken to its foundations by the assassinations of Martin Luther King Jr. and Robert Kennedy. The murder of the civil rights leader led to rioting in more than one hundred American cities and upheavals on almost every campus in the land. By the time the academic year began in the fall of 1968, the universities were aflame; more radical than ever before, students—and faculty members—were deaf to Kennan's plea for institutions devoted to study and reflection far from the madding crowd. In an April 20, 1969 letter to John Lukacs, Kennan expressed a deep sadness. "I feel quite crushed in spirit over what I read about student disorders in our universities. . . . I think this is the end—for a long time to come—of any real higher education in our country."

In August 1969, 400,000 young people descended on a dairy farm in Bethel, New York, some forty miles from Woodstock. They came for what was labeled "An Aquarian Exposition: 3 Days of Peace & Music" but was in fact a rain-soaked orgy of drugs, sex, and rock music. As we have seen, few people were as opposed as Kennan was to wars that had nothing to do with the national interest, but he rejected "peace" as a slogan and pacifism as a creed. He once explained to a gathering of Quakers that man's demonic side could ultimately be restrained only by force. Violence, he said, was the tribute we pay to original sin.

In the fall of 1968, Americans chose Richard Nixon as their president, and when, four years later, he scored a crushing reelection victory over student-supported George McGovern, hopes of imminent revolution dimmed. Still, if they could not have apocalypse now, radical students could console themselves with the thought that they might have it incrementally. That is where Antonio Gramsci came in; the Italian communist, who had spent years in Benito Mussolini's prisons, had advanced the theory that revolution would come once radicals had established "cultural hegemony," or control over society's cultural/intellectual life. The German student leader Rudi Dutschke reformulated Gramsci's idea as "the long march through the institutions"—very much including the universities.

On January 27, 1973, President Nixon signed an agreement to end the war in Vietnam, and, on the same day, suspended the draft—permanently as things turned out. As a result, radicals lost all interest in Vietnam and as a whole demonstrated little concern for the "boat people" who fled the country by sea. As Kennan had surmised, the end of the war and the draft turned restless youths to other causes. Despite the changes wrought by the Civil Rights Act of 1964, for example, students made it clear that they would not rest until the last vestige of discrimination against Black Americans was eliminated. The Revolution was to be permanent. It was not long before sixties radicals were ready to enter the academic profession, and many of them did. These "tenured radicals'" principal responsibility, as they conceived of it, was to radicalize the next generation, and they have achieved a great deal of success. As Kennan surmised, they began to collect new causes: feminism, animal rights, homosexual rights, Latino rights, Native American rights, Muslim rights, illegal immigrant rights, transgender rights.

Students, having little or no opportunity to hear a dissenting word, are easily persuaded. They refuse to permit any open challenge, shouting down dissenters or accusing them of racism, sexism, homophobia, or hate speech (examples can be found daily on the websites Campus Reform and The College Fix). Students and faculty members who would welcome debate soon discover that it is prudent to remain silent. It is the sixties redivivus, but far more radical. Speech that raises any objection to the official dogma, must not be allowed to be free. Meanwhile, serious study is severely diminished and much revolves around political activism. In his reply to the sixties radicals, Kennan had quite seriously suggested that the majority of the young enroll at a university of distinctive design, one devoted to "the breathless and backgroundless preoccupation with, and action upon, the passing scene. Its curriculum would be one uninterrupted current affairs course, consisting primarily of off-campus field work, participation in demonstrations, social work, political organizational activity, etc."

That is precisely the design of contemporary universities. With few exceptions they are what one academy president described with pride as "the engaged university." He did not mean engaged in scholarly study and research but in efforts to reconstruct the social order. Classes that present little opportunity to further that end find no place in the curriculum. One searches university catalogues in vain, for example, for a course in European diplomatic history similar to that which Kennan took with Raymond Sontag, while there are plenty focused on colonialism and its evils, real and imagined. In many schools students can major in English Literature without ever reading Shakespeare. Authors judged to be politically unreliable (Hemingway—too masculine and too white) are not only not taught, but placed on a secular Index Librorum Prohibitorum. At Princeton University Classics students no longer have to demonstrate competence in Greek and/or Latin. Classrooms are largely indoctrination centers light years away from those of the pre-1960s—to say nothing of Kennan's almost medieval institution.

It is not only on campuses that censorship and threats force students and faculty into silence or support of the official ideology. A new and far more dangerous form of McCarthyism holds sway throughout American society. Kennan was an outspoken critic of the senator and his methods but he recognized where the real danger lay. "McCarthy had no police forces. The American courts remained almost totally unaffected. . . . The entire McCarthyist phenomenon was . . . markedly nonviolent." What McCarthy had discovered was that people could be punished just as cruelly by having their reputations ruined and their possibilities of employment reduced as by being placed under lock and key. That is exactly how contemporary McCarthyism operates. Speech that is or can be construed to be outside the bounds of acceptable thought can result in one being made a social outcast, forced to recant and to resign. In an effort to save something of their former lives, those subjected to McCarthyite tactics perform humiliating self-criticisms in the manner of the millions of victims of Mao Zedong's Cultural Revolution (1966–76). In that way, others are made aware that silence is not enough, that they must praise favored men and women, living and dead, and denounce those whom the new intellectual ruling class has judged to be unworthy.

And just as China's Red Guards destroyed historical relics, contemporary militants busy themselves with the destruction or removal of monuments and statues. "Wherever the authority of the past is too suddenly and too drastically undermined," Kennan warned a Princeton audience in 1954, "there the foundations of man's inner health and stability begin to crumble, insecurity and panic begin to take over, conduct becomes erratic and aggressive."

Kennan lived long enough to witness the decadence that had come to characterize the lives of the young—and not of theirs alone. Both Western Europe and the United States, he told George Urban, had "lost a sense of the fitness of things, and that *is* the meaning of decadence." Jacques Barzun held a similar view. In his magisterial *From Dawn to Decadence: 500 Years of Western Cultural Life, 1500 to the Present*, he instanced "getting married underground in a subway station or around a pool, in swimming suits. And since unfitness meant freedom, other conventions should be defied, notably those classed as manners."

Kennan complained often of the prevalent contempt for graciousness and good taste. He never forgot the day that he put in at a Danish port that was sponsoring a youth festival. "The place was swarming with hippies—motorbikes, girl-friends, drugs, pornography, drunkenness, noise—it was all there." In a long letter/essay that *Die Zeit* published in 1976, he held nothing back:

> Poor old West: succumbing feebly, day by day, to its own decadence, sliding into debility on the slime of its own self-indulgent permissiveness; its drugs, its crime, its pornography, its pampering of the youth, its addiction to its bodily comforts, its rampant materialism and consumerism—and then trembling before the menace of the wicked Russians. . . . This persistent externalization of the threat from without and blindness to the threat within: this is the symptom of some deep failure to come to terms with reality—and with one's self.

Emancipation, Barzun wrote, was the basic theme of Western decadence. In conscious opposition to that rallying cry, Kennan expressed wonder at the compulsive preoccupation with explicit sex that marked so much of the movie screen and the printed word. It was, as he knew, the result of the "sexual revolution" that began in the sixties and has continued unabated. Released from virtually every restraint, human nature has been found to seek degeneracy often enough to create a disorderly, hedonistic, and dangerous society. "The sexual act itself," Barzun observed, "was imitated wherever it could be managed, onstage or onscreen; some performers went so far as to commit indecent acts in front of their live audience."

"Sexual revolution," combined with the advent of the Internet has let loose a flood of easily accessed pornography. Jean-Claude Larchet cites a number of surveys to the effect that of the fifty-seven million Americans who have access to the Internet, twenty-five million visit pornographic sites for spells of between one and ten hours per week—at work as well as at home. Many thousands of these are addicted to pornographic sites and other online sexual material. "If you don't like it, don't watch" is what often passes for an argument against legal restraints of what has passed from decadence to depravity. Pornography coarsens and degrades the aesthetic and moral environment in which all of us live.

Decadence in Kennan's understanding referred to moral decay, a society and civilization in a downward spiral. For *New York Times* columnist Ross Douthat it means nothing more than a stagnant society, one unable to achieve any new breakthroughs, any real progress. One sees some fine tuning of technology, but nothing truly inventive. There is nothing fresh in the art world or in the popular culture—merely endless repetition. There are no major explorations of space. Nor is there anything new on the political horizon. Decadence means that Francis Fukuyama may have been right: liberal democracy does seem to be the "end of history." Given that no serious challenger to it has yet appeared, decadence may well be our collective fate for a very long time. But according to Douthat, there is as matters now stand no viable alternative—it is after all, "a kindly despotism" that keeps us "comfortably numb" and permits us liberties of pleasure and consumption, if not religious freedom and free speech. It is, in sum, a "sustainable decadence." If that is what now counts as a reason for encouragement, Kennan's tragic view of life was too optimistic.

After identifying many of his country's addictions, Kennan wrote that "beyond these, there are also troublesome societal conditions: attitudes of hopelessness, skepticism, cynicism, and bewilderment, particularly among the youth—that have led many observers to characterize this society (and, I think, not unjustly) as a 'sick' one." He attributed those social pathologies primarily to a loss of, or indifference to, the Christian faith. As a result of personal experience and historical study, he could cite as a warning the example of nineteenth- and twentieth-century Russia. Atheism was at the core of the revolutionary movements that eventually brought down the tsarist government, as it was of the Soviet regime, which did everything in its power not merely to destroy the Russian Orthodox Church but to eradicate Christianity. As Solzhenitsyn made clear, that effort ultimately failed, but it did engender hopelessness, cynicism, and moral compromises that all but destroyed the lives of millions.

During his year at Balliol College, Oxford, Kennan was alarmed "at the prevailing absence not only of a conscious faith but even of any visible interest in religion among a people the foundations of whose greatness rested on the bedrock of the Christian Church; and, conversely, at the prevalence of what struck me as an uncritical spirit of egalitarianism and materialism."

Kennan recognized that America too was a secular nation that, for the most part, did not take Christianity seriously. That he was alarmed by that irreligion is evidenced by his many talks in churches around Princeton, the Christian services he conducted in Yugoslavia, and his oft-stated admiration for Christians such as Helmuth James von Moltke and Boris Pasternak. He went out of his way, even in talks on foreign policy, to inform the members of his audience that he was himself a Christian. At the same time, however, he insisted that it was a sacrilege to confuse the prospering of the United States as a political entity with the fulfillment of God's purposes for the human race. One wonders how he would have reacted to Yale professor David Gelernter's book of 2007, *Americanism: The Fourth Great Western Religion*.

The "sacrilege" of which Kennan spoke is woven like a common thread throughout the fabric of the nation's history. From the beginning, Americans have imagined themselves to be a new chosen people in a new promised land with a millenarian destiny. As Walter McDougall has pointed out, "By prohibiting Congress from establishing any particular religion, [the First Amendment to the Constitution] silently established a civil religion to which all sectarian believers must bow." Despite Kennan's censure, that civil religion has continued to conflate the sacred and secular—no more openly than in America's oft-repeated claim to be a "city on a hill." The metaphor comes from Jesus's Sermon on the Mount (St. Matthew 5:14): "Ye are the light of the world. A city that is set on an hill cannot be hid." He referred to His disciples, not to America.

President Reagan was so fond of the metaphor that he made of it "a *shining* city on a hill." But Richard Gamble is right to point out that his image was "utterly secular, consisting of no more than a bustling, tolerant commercial enterprise—a Scottish Enlightenment vision closer to Adam Smith than Jesus." His was a civil religion whose god remains largely anonymous. Anyone but an atheist, according to Gamble, could picture his own god during a presidential inauguration or a Fourth of July celebration. Perhaps the most explicit integration of the sacred and the secular is to be found in the *American Patriot's Bible*. "Patriot stands with Patriarch, Decalogue with Declaration, Noah with Noah Webster. It is all one story."

The *American Patriot's Bible* would not have pleased Kennan. The church's responsibility, he believed, was not to promote American messianism, but to teach man "to walk in God's ways, to extend to him the comfort of the sacraments, to support him in his moments of weakness, to console him in his failures, to teach him how to bear the heaviest of his sorrows, to maintain him in the strength of his belief."

Without that belief, Kennan feared that, quoting Dostoevsky, "everything is permitted." At the very least, it had become clear to him that with the decline of religious influence, moral standards had eroded. The question is, he wrote in 1985, "whether there is any such thing as morality that does not rest, consciously or otherwise, on some foundation of religious faith; for the renunciation of self-interest, which is what all morality implies, can never be rationalized by purely secular and materialistic considerations." Impressive attempts have been made to find a nonreligious foundation, above all, perhaps, Immanuel Kant's "categorical imperative." But few people have read *Groundwork of the Metaphysics of Morals* and fewer still have understood it. The social pathologies that Kennan catalogued are difficult to explain other than as the result of secularization.

8

For a Representative Government

In his conversation with George Urban, Kennan characterized himself as "a strange mixture of a reactionary and a liberal." For most moderns, *reactionary* is a pejorative term signaling a stubborn opposition to progress, as they define it. To favor reaction, let us be clear, is to hold that the past boasted times that were superior to the present. If that is not true, being a reactionary is an unworthy profession; if it is true, however, reactionaries should be praised, not censured. We know that Kennan did indeed judge the past, the eighteenth century, to be preferable to the modern world. And, by extension, he ranked traditional conservative authoritarian governments—nondespotic and nonideological in nature—higher than democracies.

Despite what many of his contemporaries had been led to believe, Kennan insisted that there were fundamental differences between totalitarian and authoritarian governments. The former—Nazi Germany and communist Russia—were in his judgment aberrations, historically unrecognizable forms of government; neither Plato nor Aristotle knew of them. "These regimes," he pointed out in *Around the Cragged Hill*, "differed in certain essential respects from all the other variations of government that the history of Western civilization has to offer." They were unalike not only in the dimensions of their cruelties, but "in the fact that the victims of those cruelties were in overwhelming proportion, the innocent rather than the guilty."

Authoritarian governments, on the other hand, were far more common in history than democracies, and unlike totalitarian regimes they maintained order without destroying liberty or imposing a political religion. What is more, he wrote in a 1959 piece for *The Atlantic Monthly*, "the authoritarian regime, despite its origins and its sanctions, often rests on a wide area of popular acceptance and reflects popular aspirations in important degree." It is usually, that is, looked on as legitimate.

Kennan had firsthand knowledge of authoritarian governments. He was in Vienna in 1935 while recuperating from a bout with ulcers and admired the manner in which the government of Austrian Chancellor Kurt von Schuschnigg, drawing on the advice of experts rather than of members of parliament or the populace, went about its business. He was later to describe that government as "conservative, semi-fascist, but still moderate" and to complain that those in the West who criticized it found it difficult to distinguish between traditional conservatives and Nazis.

For Western liberals, Kennan told his Oxford audience in 1957–58, Czechoslovakia, not Austria, was "the darling." That was so because Czechoslovak president Tomáš Masaryk presided over the only democratic state in interwar Eastern Europe. That also explained why Westerners tended to pass over Austria's downfall and to identify the demise of Czechoslovakia as the great turning point in European affairs generally, and in Soviet policy in particular. In Kennan's judgment, Stalin regarded the *Anschluss*—the forced union of Austria with Germany—as of far greater significance.

On February 12, 1938, Schuschnigg traveled to Hitler's *Berghof*, near Berchtesgaden, in an effort to reduce friction with Nazi Germany. To his shock and dismay, he found himself surrounded by German military leaders and a Führer who had no intension of conducting negotiations. He threatened to invade Austria unless Schuschnigg gave the Austrian Nazi Party freedom of action and placed its leaders in strategic government posts. In the hope of averting armed conquest, Schuschnigg ultimately acquiesced to the demands. One month later, on March 12, Hitler occupied and quickly annexed Austria. Later in the same year, Kennan composed a paper (never published) entitled "The Prerequisites: Notes on Problems of the United States in 1938," in which he argued for changes in his own country leading to an "authoritarian state," much like that of Schuschnigg's Austria.

Pre-Anschluss Austria was not the only authoritarian government that Kennan admired. Shortly before Labor Day, 1943, he received orders to proceed to neutral Portugal, where, among other duties, he was to secure Allied use of naval ports and air landings in the Azores, islands extending some five hundred miles in the Atlantic. The mission demanded much of his energy because of his own government's imperious attitude toward Portuguese neutrality and sovereignty, jealously guarded by Prime Minister António de Oliveira Salazar.

In its obituary (1970), the *New York Times* described Salazar as ascetic, aloof, professorial, and understated. A bachelor, he led a quiet, austere life away from the public and "politics." Dean Acheson once praised him as a "remarkable man, the nearest approach in our time to Plato's philosopher-king." Devoted to the Catholic Church, Salazar attended a Jesuit seminary before earning degrees in economics and law. He entered public life in 1926 as finance minister before becoming prime minister in 1932; it was a position he held until 1968. His rule was authoritarian but neither despotic nor ideological, and he gave his country long years of economic and political stability.

Of Salazar, Kennan quickly formed a favorable opinion. "I am convinced," he wrote in an official letter of December 11, 1944, that "Salazar, operating on a set of principles which are quite different from our own principles of democracy, has created and maintained conditions of life far more credible and acceptable to the psychology of the people than the conditions which prevailed there under a theoretically democratic and republican form of government prior to his advent to power." He recognized in Salazar a traditional authoritarian, not a fascist revolutionary. Never did the strongman adopt the trappings of fascism—chanting crowds, mass meetings, the cult of personality.

A fascist dictatorship, Salazar once said, leaned "towards a pagan Caesarism, towards a new state which recognizes no limitations of legal or moral order." He recognized too the similarities between international and national socialism: "Although Fascism and National Socialism differ from Communism in economic outlook and ideas, they are alike in their conception of the totalitarian state." And he did, after all, sympathize with Great Britain and lease bases to the Allies.

Like the authoritarian leaders whom he respected, Kennan looked with distaste on mass politics. "For years," he wrote in the late 1960s, "Gibbon's dictum 'Under a democratical government the citizens exercise the powers of sovereignty; and those powers will be first abased and afterwards lost, if they are committed to an unwieldy multitude' has lain at the heart of my political philosophy." He shared the views of José Ortega y Gasset, the Spanish liberal who made an important distinction between mass men and select individuals, between those who demand little or nothing of themselves and those who demand much. It was men of the former sort, according to Ortega, who were asserting their right to mediocrity and who attempted to crush everything outstanding, excellent, and noble.

While serving in Berlin in 1940, Kennan inherited from Alexander Kirk, the departing *chargé d'affaires*, a clandestine contact with Count Helmuth von Moltke, a great-grandnephew of the legendary Prussian field marshal. Moltke had been drafted by the Abwehr (military intelligence) to act as an adviser concerning international law, and it did not take him long to learn the extent of Nazi lawlessness. At about the same time as his first meetings with Kennan, he and Count Peter Yorck von Wartenburg formed what the Gestapo labeled the Kreisau Circle of opponents of the Nazi regime. Meeting in Berlin or at Moltke's family estate in Kreisau, Silesia (now Krzyżowa, Poland), members of the circle, some twenty in number, occupied various stations in society—they were united by their hopes for a new, post–Third Reich, Germany.

Moltke was a profoundly conservative man, and precisely for that reason he welcomed into his circle a number of undogmatic socialists, who, like him, believed that Germany would have to drink the full cup of defeat before it could begin to renew its moral and spiritual life. His was above all a civilizational resistance to a barbarism that could not be uprooted by assassinating Hitler, something he opposed as a matter of principle in any case. For him, as the late German historian Joachim Fest pointed out, mass society was the great scourge of the time; he was appalled by egalitarianism and favored an authoritarianism disciplined, according to Kennan, by "a deep religious faith—a vision of Christianity broad, tolerant, and all-embracing, like that of

Pasternak, in the range of its charity." Arrested by the Gestapo on January 19, 1944, Moltke was hanged in Plötzensee prison on January 23, 1945.

Moltke exercised a deep and lasting influence on Kennan. In his memoirs, the American wrote that the martyred German "has remained for me over the intervening years a pillar of moral conscience and an unfailing source of political and intellectual inspiration." He reinforced Kennan's principled opposition to mass democracy and his admiration for the old-fashioned authoritarianism represented by upper-class opponents of the Nazi regime. So strong, Kennan wrote in 1973, was the unwillingness of Western-liberal historians "to concede to these people any serious merit, or even sympathy, that one gains the impression of a certain real irritation, as though the persons in question had had the ill grace, before dying in their various forms of agony, to confuse the issue by disturbing an otherwise tidy pattern of unadulterated German iniquity."

Moltke was aware that the new Germany for which he worked could not mean a return to the Wilhelmian era. On August 9, 1943, therefore, he drafted a prospective constitution according to which eligible voters, all persons over twenty-one, would elect members of municipal and county assemblies. They in turn would elect members of the provincial legislature, who would then elect members of the Reichstag. It would, in short, be a representative government.

In the same vein, Kennan recognized that the historical experience of his own country ruled out any authoritarian system of government. At the same time, he could never reconcile himself to the "permissive excesses" of an egalitarian democracy. It was, then, as a conservative liberal, indebted to "the great philosophical insights of such men as Burke and Tocqueville," that he concluded that there was only one other possibility for a reasonably good government. In a diary entry of June 11, 1986, he identified it:

> I am a firm believer (as I believe most of the founding fathers of our country were) in *representative* government, as opposed to government by plebiscite, by acclamation, or by direct action of the public. The public is not supposed to know, indeed, cannot know, how best to decide the many questions that come before a government. That, as Burke so eloquently argued, is the task of representatives, and particularly those who are able to give to problems of government their undivided attention, and they should use their own judgment in making the decisions.

Kennan was referring to Burke's famous speech of November 3, 1774, to the Electors of Bristol, on the occasion of his election as one of that city's representatives in Parliament. In view of their historical importance, beauty of expression, and influence on Kennan, the key sections of that speech deserve to be quoted at some length. "It ought to be the happiness and glory of a representative to live in the strictest union, the closest correspondence, and the most unreserved communication with his constituents. Their wishes ought to have great weight with him; their opinion, high respect; their business, unremitted attention. It is his duty to sacrifice his repose, his pleasures, his satisfactions, to theirs; and above all, ever, and in all cases, to prefer their interest to his own."

Burke then continued. "But his unbiased opinion, his mature judgment, his enlightened conscience, he ought not to sacrifice to you, to any man, or to any set of men living. These he does not derive from your pleasure; no, nor from the law and the constitution. They are a trust from Providence, for the abuse of which he is deeply answerable."

Kennan entitled an important section of *Around the Cragged Hill* "Plebiscite versus Representative Government." In the latter, he reminded (or informed) his readers, laws were to be drawn up and adopted by a representative legislative body elected by the citizenry for that purpose. With that act of election, the public's active involvement in the legislative process was substantially completed. "God forbid," he wrote to John Lukacs, "that it should ever itself attempt to rule." If citizens disliked what their representative was doing, they were free to criticize him (or her) and, all else failing, elect someone else.

The representative was not under any obligation to poll his constituents and then cast his vote in accord with the result—in which case a secretary alone would be required. While taking the will of his constituents into account, the representative was expected to exercise his personal judgment in arriving at his decisions. Plebiscitary democracy, Kennan pointed out, negates the principle of the elected representative's personal responsibility in favor of an irresponsible and anonymous power. It completely ignores the fact that the public may, for a wide variety of reasons, be mistaken in its (majority) opinion. That opinion, when solicited by pollsters, can easily be, and usually is, manipulated by the very phrasing of the questions asked; nor is any opportunity given to those polled to qualify their replies ("yes, but," "only if"). Polls are in fact primarily designed to form public opinion, not to reflect it.

We recall that the Marquis de Custine had gone to Russia "to seek arguments against representative government"—but returned "the partisan of constitutions." In his study of the marquis, Kennan cited the explanation for his change of heart with evident appreciation—because it mirrored his own views. "I left France scared by the abuses of a false liberty; I return to my country persuaded that if, logically speaking, the representative system is not the most moral form of government, it is, practically, the most wise and moderate; preserving the people on the one side from democratic license, and on the other, from the most glaring abuses of despotism; I therefore ask myself if we ought not to impose a silence upon our antipathies, and submit without murmur to a necessary policy, and one which, after all, brings to nations prepared for it, more good than evil."

That was, Kennan clearly believed, a lesson well learned, but he regretted the fact that Custine was unable to foresee one of the most important developments in Russian history in the years leading up to the revolution. That history was destined to be determined by the competing efforts of three forces: the diehards who wanted no change at all; the liberals and moderate socialists who wanted gradual reform and peaceful, organic progress; and the revolutionary socialists and anarchists who wanted violent, sudden change. Kennan pointed out that there was a common bond of purpose between the first and third categories—neither wanted the tsarist regime to evolve in the direction of a greater degree of representation. The liberals alone pursued that objective.

Among the three forces, Custine was able to see the first clearly and to sense the third dimly. In Kennan's judgment, however, he was oblivious to the existence, and future achievements, of Russian liberalism. As he had written to Princeton University professor C. E. Black in 1955, "It seems to me that there is a pronounced tendency in this country to ignore or forget the changes that were occurring in Russia between 1861 and 1917, and to portray Russia as a country which was suddenly transformed by the revolution from a state of utter cultural, economic, and political backwardness into one oriented, however crudely, to the modern age."

Kennan had in mind the 1861 abolition of serfdom, the 1864 establishment of *zemstvos* (organs of local self-government whose deputies were chosen by de facto electoral colleges), the reform of the judicial system, the loosening of the constraints of censorship, the agrarian reforms of Pyotr Stolypin, and the establishment of a Duma or parliament, albeit with limited powers. Every bit as important in Kennan's view was the flourishing of one of the greatest cultures in the annals of human history. These promising developments were aborted by the war and revolution.

Kennan was, like Solzhenitsyn, particularly impressed by Stolypin, the prime minister hated by the Russian left and the right. "Stolypin had grace and style in everything he did," he told a Princeton University audience in 1964. "The center of [Prime Minister Sergei] Witte's attention was industry. With Stolypin it was agriculture." What is more, he "concentrated his attention on the need for *internal* reform."

Stolypin outlined a plan to turn the peasants' allotment of land in the commune (*mir*) into permanent (private) property. Transforming peasants into smallholders was, he was convinced, the key to their prosperity and allegiance to the tsarist government. In accord with a decree of November 9, 1907, the Russian peasant obtained the right to leave the commune, consolidate his allotment as a private holding, or if he pleased, separate himself completely from the village and set up a farm with its own house.

Unfortunately for Russia, Stolypin was assassinated in 1911, and that altered the course of Russian history. In Kennan's view, events such as that demonstrated history's radical contingency. "It is a reasonable view," he observed, "that the Russian Revolution was fortuitous, insofar as it was the product of a number of factors in the sudden coming-together of which no logical pattern can be discerned. One can think of a number of individual circumstances any one of which might very easily, but for the hand of chance, have been quite different than it actually was—and different in such a way as to obviate the second Russian Revolution of 1917, if not the first."

Kennan knew that the Founding Fathers of the United States conceived their political system to be that of a representative government. As he once told John Lukacs: "If I thought that this—'representative government'—was to be the pattern for the new age, I would be less skeptical of its future. . . . But in the United States, I fear, the trends are in the other directions." He meant in the direction of ever-increasing democratization. "Many years ago," he told George Urban, "I fell to thinking about the election of our Senators, and I recalled that initially they were meant to be appointed by the State governors, and I was thinking that would still be the best way to have them selected."

He was right. According to Article I, section 3 of the US Constitution, "The Senate of the United States shall be composed of two Senators from each State, chosen by the Legislature thereof for six years." However, the Seventeenth Amendment to the Constitution (1913) transferred the election of senators from state legislatures to the people directly. It marked an important stage in the ongoing movement to democratize, that is to destroy, the representative system that the Founders created. Unlike members of the House of Representatives, who were elected by the people directly, members of the Senate were elected by the people indirectly. Placed beyond immediate popular reach, senators were able to deliberate with greater independence and to speak with greater candor.

In *Democracy in America*, Tocqueville wrote that when he entered the US House of Representatives, he was struck by "the vulgar demeanor of that great assembly. Often there is not a distinguished man in the whole number. . . . They are mostly village lawyers, men in trade, or even persons belonging to the

lower classes of society." In the Senate, on the other hand, he en-
countered "a large proportion of the celebrated men of America.
Scarcely an individual is to be seen in it who has not had an active
and illustrious career: the Senate is composed of eloquent advocates, distinguished generals, wise magistrates, and statesmen of
note, whose arguments would do honor to the most remarkable
parliamentary debates of Europe."

In opposing the proposed amendment, Elihu Root, the Republican senator from New York who had been awarded the Nobel
Prize for Peace in 1912, described the senators of his own day, or
at least some of them, as elder statesmen who had attained the respect of their fellow citizens and who were willing to undertake the
responsibilities of public office without seeking them; men who
would accept the burden as a patriotic duty, but would not subject
themselves to the labor and strife of a political campaign. Root was
describing himself and, without knowing it, George Kennan.

As Kennan knew, the men, or in more recent years the women,
who entered the Senate by direct election were, by and large,
a lesser breed—Huey Long and Joseph McCarthy rather than
Henry Clay, Daniel Webster, and John C. Calhoun. That is why,
in *Around the Cragged Hill*, he recommended to his countrymen
the creation of a Council of State that would stand outside of politics and whose members would consider long-term problems and,
after careful deliberation, offer policy suggestions. Members of
the council would be persons of high distinction and independent
judgment—they would be what senators once were.

As aware as Kennan was of senatorial decline, he seemed not
to know that by the time the Seventeenth Amendment gained
the required approval of two-thirds of the Senate (voting concur-
rently with two-thirds of the House) and three-fourths of the state
legislatures, the democratic die had already been cast. As C. H.

Hoebeke has shown in convincing detail, the democratization of the American political system commenced early in the nation's life. The House initially proposed the direct election of senators in 1826, and there were many more efforts in that direction after that, leading to President Andrew Johnson's plea before Congress in 1868. In 1906, William Randolph Hearst's *Cosmopolitan* magazine ran a nine-part series of articles entitled "The Treason of the Senate." Written by David Graham Phillips, the series attacked the practice of some senators of rewarding their campaign contributors.

Although Phillips's charges were often exaggerated and earned him President Theodore Roosevelt's contempt as a "muckraker" (from "the Man with the Muck-rake" in John Bunyan's *Pilgrim's Progress*), they accelerated the push for reform. In 1907, Oregon pioneered direct election; Nebraska soon followed suit. It was 1913 before the amendment was finally ratified, but by then the Senate was an all-but-popular assembly. By mandating the direct primary nomination of Senate candidates, to whom they then pledged themselves as voters for the Senate, state legislators had created de facto, if technically still indirect, popular elections to that once high office.

In *Democracy: An American Novel*, Henry Adams, a Kennan favorite, provided a devastating portrait of a US senator of his time—Silas P. Ratcliffe (the historical James G. Blaine) of Illinois. The novel revolves around Ratcliffe's efforts to win the hand of Mrs. Lightfoot Lee, a widow who has come to Washington with an eye to gaining some understanding of democracy in practice; she is Adams himself. "Do you," she asks one of her acquaintances, "think democracy the best government, and universal suffrage a success?" Initially drawn to Ratcliffe because of his political skills and his proud boast that the pleasure of politics lay in the possession of power, she eventually recognizes that he has led her to lose sight of the distinction between right and wrong.

Ratcliffe not only admits, but affirms that his actions are determined not by principle but by power; his only principle is the want of principles. In politics, he tells Mrs. Lee, we cannot keep our hands clean. And he doesn't. He accepts bribes, orchestrates voter fraud, attends church only because he needs the votes of those of his constituents who are churchgoers, and pursues any and every avenue that will lead to the presidency. In the end, Mrs. Lee awakens from the trance into which Ratcliffe had placed her, rejects his insistent proposal of marriage, and leaves Washington. Throughout the novel, Adams makes it clear that Ratcliffe is the symbol not only of senatorial corruption but of democracy itself.

The Electoral College is the indirect method by which, in principle, the president of the United States is elected. In Federalist No. 68, Alexander Hamilton promoted the plan of having the people choose electors for the special and limited purpose of electing the president. "A small number of persons," according to Hamilton, "selected by their fellow-citizens from the general mass, will be most likely to possess [the requisite] information and discernment. It was also peculiarly desirable to afford as little opportunity as possible to tumult and disorder." The number of those chosen was to be equal to the number of senators and representatives of each state.

The election of the president, like the election of senators, was overtaken by advocates of democracy early in its existence. Electors do not, in fact, exercise their own judgment when deciding for one candidate or another; in the vast majority of cases, they vote for the candidate receiving the largest popular vote in their state (in thirty-three states and the District of Columbia there are laws against a "faithless elector," one who does not cast his vote for the candidate of the party for whom he pledged to vote). Because, however, it is possible for a candidate to win the national popular vote and lose the electoral vote (as happened in the 1876, 1888, 2000, and 2016 elections), the democracy lobbies unceasingly for the elimination of the college.

Constitution changes are the work of those whom Burke called the constitution mongers. Between 1789 and 1848, the people in their respective states adopted thirty-six new constitutions, an unwieldy means of change that soon gave way to amending existing constitutions. For understandable reasons, the American people had come to believe that the Constitution was a democratic document, and when it failed to work in an egalitarian manner they concluded that the Constitution, not their belief in its character, had to be changed. There are now twenty-seven amendments to the Constitution and insistent demands for more—most recently the Equal Rights Amendment (ERA), according to which "equality of rights under the law shall not be denied or abridged by the United States or by any state on account of sex." With each amendment the United States moves further away from the representative government that the Founders crafted and that Kennan defended.

Kennan argued that the generations subsequent to that of the framers of the Constitution had perverted what was supposed to be a representative government into a boss ridden democracy. He believed too that this unfortunate transformation could be attributed largely to the country's acceptance of universal suffrage. In a diary entry of July 9, 1970, he wrote that "in the broad spectrum of political institutions running all the way from the usurping tyrant to the egalitarian democracy, there is only one segment that yields reasonably good government. It is one that combines . . . continuity with the existence of an influential upper class whose

composition is made up largely by inheritance but partly by re-
cruitment of able people from other inherited stations, its influence assured by some sort of limited franchise or weighted voting,
particularly in national affairs."

By the mid-1830s, just as *Democracy in America* was about
to appear, every one of the original states had adopted the all-
(white) male standard. They replaced property qualifications for
voting by the paying of taxes, which was supplanted in turn by
mere residence requirements of ever-shorter duration. Eventually the exclusion of women and Black Americans came to a justifiable end—but so did the existence of *any* voter qualification
(or any proof of qualification). Tocqueville explained why that
was bound to happen: "When a nation begins to modify the elective qualification . . . sooner or later that qualification will be
entirely abolished."

The reason was that the further electoral rights are extended,
the greater is the need of extending them: "After each concession
the strength of the democracy increases, and its demands increase
with its strength. The ambition of those who are below the appointed rate is irritated in exact proportion to the great number
of those who are above it. The exception at last becomes the rule,
concession follows concession, and no stop can be made short of
universal suffrage."

That the representative government framed by the Founders
was superior to the mass democracy that has replaced it was one
of Kennan's principal teachings. It was, however, a lesson that his
countrymen were unlikely to take to heart, egalitarianism being
for them an article of religious faith. Representative government
was undoubtedly a case of inequality because it meant that representatives could deliberate and vote on matters that the mass

of people could not. That was the whole point. People might well be able to arrive at reasoned judgments regarding local matters; a PhD in political science is not necessary in order to arrive at an informed opinion about the wisdom of, say, preserving a city park or constructing a new housing complex. To judge matters concerning foreign policy, however, requires something more than the ability to open a Twitter account.

Before dismissing Kennan's brief for representative government out of hand, his countrymen would do well to reflect on the fact that democracies are invariably ruled by elites able to master the art of propaganda, the art of achieving and maintaining power by manipulating public opinion. With so many means of persuasion at their disposal, elites can almost always isolate themselves from serious challenge. That means that The People do not actually rule; they are only made to believe that they do by ambitious men and women. Representatives elected indirectly would be better able to resist public pressures manufactured by self-interested politicians and those, particularly in the media, who do their bidding.

Kennan would not be surprised by the reluctance his countrymen have shown to heed his warnings and learn his lessons. His was, as we know, a tragic sense of life. And yet he never tired in his efforts to open the eyes of others and stopped short of counseling despair. As the epigraph for the epilogue to *Around the Cragged Hill*, he chose the words of the wizard Gandalf in J.R.R. Tolkien's *Fellowship of the Ring*: "Despair is only for those who see the end beyond all doubt."

However pessimistic Kennan was concerning the future of his country, and of Western civilization in general, his Christian faith made him tremble at the thought of destroying all hope among his readers. "If the commentator's words sow despair . . . he may, by his despairing words, have given discouragement where courage is needed." That, Kennan concluded, would be "the unpardonable sin. The hour may be late, but there is nothing that says that it is too late." The lessons that he hoped would bear fruit he had offered "with a view to encouraging others to take heart—not to lose it."

Conclusion

WHY KENNAN STILL MATTERS

George Kennan died on March 17, 2005. Since then the warnings he issued and the counsel he offered have become even more essential. His plea for a mature, that is, a realist, foreign policy has largely fallen on deaf ears. There have been challenges to "the Blob," but realists, representing the principal alternative, remain a minority shunned by think tanks and the media. The foreign policy elite is still made up of neoconservatives and liberal internationalists protective of their power and influence. Far from conducting foreign policy on the basis of the national interest and a balance of power, they continue to promote ideological (democratizing) interventions. Any foreign government charged with having failed the tests of democracy and human rights is regarded as a legitimate target for either armed intervention or public castigation coupled with the leveling of sanctions. A moderate and restrained policy remains the distant hope of a few knowledgeable and experienced observers.

Of what Kennan described as America's "unfortunate involvement" in the Near East, there is as yet no end. As of May 2021, there were still 2,500 US troops in Iraq, and although the Iraqi government was able to reach an accord with the United States with respect to the withdrawal of combat forces, no date was set. In the same month, President Joseph Biden announced the complete withdrawal of the 2,500 US troops from Afghanistan by September 11, 2021—but in the event the date turned out not to be his to set. On August 15, Taliban forces captured Kabul, the Afghan capital; so sudden was the collapse of the 300,000-man Afghan army (and its government) that the Biden administration did not know, or would not say, how many Americans remained in the country—or how they planned to evacuate them. Far worse, as chaotic efforts to evacuate at least some were in process, ISIS suicide bombers killed at least ninety people, including at least thirteen American servicemen, at the Kabul airport.

After twenty years, the longest war in American history, the cost in blood and treasure was staggering. Some 2,500 US servicemen, together with 47,000 Afghan civilians, lost their lives. The United States spent more than $2 trillion on the war and $300 billion on the care of casualties—with another half-trillion to come. (ABC News projects that by 2050, the cost of interest alone on the Afghan war debt will reach $6.5 trillion.) It was precisely because he foresaw the possibility of such a disaster that Kennan told his diary on November 21, 2001, that "regarding the war in Afghanistan I find myself more of an isolationist than ever."

More disturbing, had Kennan lived to witness it, is the all but complete deterioration of relations with Russia; scarcely a day passes without some member of government or the media describing that land as a hostile power that must be taught to behave, although how that would be done without risking a nuclear war is left unexplained. In an article he wrote shortly after the collapse of the Soviet Union, Kennan signaled his distress at the Western media's suspicions of the new Russia and made it clear that democracy, as Americans understand it, should not be expected of the post-Soviet government. Yet US government leaders and media outlets continue to demand it.

That has been particularly so since President Putin rose to power. The list of reasons that Putin's American critics cite for demonizing him grows ever longer—he hopes to restore the Soviet Union, he is Stalin, he is Hitler, he is a KGB thug and murderer, he is corrupt, he is a fascist and white supremacist, he meddles in US elections, he is an expansionist. That is quite an indictment but none of the particulars, as the late Stephen F. Cohen pointed out in *War With Russia?* is credible; instead, that distinguished student of Russian affairs praised Putin as the most consequential statesman of the twenty-first century.

Nevertheless, President Trump, against what may well have been his better judgment, imposed a series of sanctions on Russia, and President Biden, unwilling to acknowledge Russia's legitimate security interests in its own region, seems prepared to go to war over her conflicts with Ukraine—a land that few Americans can locate on a map. To do so would likely require reliance on air forces or even tactical nuclear weapons; should the Russians then respond, there would be ominous consequences for the entire world. That is precisely what Kennan feared and about which he cautioned again and again. Even when Stalin was in power, he thought it possible, indeed necessary, to prevent disagreements with Russia from escalating into an all-out war. He saw no reason not to maintain friendly relations with a Russia that was democratic in the Russian understanding of the term; no fundamental interests were likely to clash. Unfortunately, the US foreign policy establishment is invested in the idea that Russia poses a threat of almost world-historic magnitude.

Kennan's attitude toward China never varied. In a diary entry dated November 25, 1996, he described the Middle Kingdom as the seat of a great culture that deserved the highest respect. Its people, in his judgment, were highly intelligent, even if xenophobic.

He believed that the United States would be wise to "treat them on the diplomatic level with the most impeccable courtesy (which they would understand) but to have, beyond that, as little as possible to do with them." American businesses would be well-advised to avoid any extensive dependence on China even if that should mean missed economic opportunities. Most important, he urged the US government to "desist, finally and completely, from any and every effort to press the Chinese government, now or in future, in matters of human rights. That is their concern, not ours."

Kennan's admonitions have been ignored. In the summer of 2021, the United States, together with other members of the G-7 (Canada, France, Germany, Italy, Japan, and the UK) issued a statement insisting that China "respect human rights and fundamental freedoms, especially in relation to Xinjiang [home to the Uyghur Muslims] and those rights, freedoms and high degree of autonomy for Hong Kong." The government of President Xi Jinping's brutal treatment of the Uyghurs and Christians is no secret but, as Kennan noted repeatedly, the US government is not in a position to force an end to practices, however repugnant, in foreign countries; noninterference in the internal affairs of another country was a long-standing principle of American diplomacy. For the United States, the domestic character of a government is less important than its international behavior—witness its wartime alliance with Stalin's tyrannical regime.

The respect that Kennan urged the United States to show for China would certainly include a recognition that, as a rising power, it had legitimate interests in areas of the world within its sphere of influence. That includes Taiwan; the island is not of strategic importance to the United States, which makes it unwise to guarantee its defense. There is no question that Kennan would have regarded China's military threat, as opposed to its economic and technological challenges, as exaggerated as that of the Soviet Union, especially in view of the fact that US military spending is far greater than that of China.

Although the US foreign policy elite is, for reasons that call for investigation, far less hostile to China than to Russia, there has been talk in government and the media of "holding China accountable" for the probable release of the coronavirus from a research laboratory in the city of Wuhan. What, one can only wonder, do they propose? A threat of war? Such a war, if it came to a "nuclear exchange," would be suicidal for the United States and calamitous for humanity. Based on what he said repeatedly, we have a good idea what Kennan would have counseled: maintain proper, if distant, relations and hope that, over time, China might modify its behavior.

In a diary entry of March 21, 1977, Kennan wrote that "the years 2000 to 2050 should witness the end of the great Western civilization. The Chinese, more prudent and less spoiled, no less given to over-population but prepared to be more ruthless in the control of its effects, may inherit the ruins." Those were prophetic words, occasioned by his recognition that American society was heading for the abyss.

As early as 1975, Kennan warned of the deterioration of life in American cities. That was years before the violence and looting that broke out across the land in the summer of 2020. He did not predict the tent cities of the homeless or the war on police officers, but he would not have been greatly surprised. He deplored urban life and would have been chagrined by the fact that small towns are evolving into cities and replicating big-city pathologies. Industrialization, which he also deplored, may be in decline in the United States, but it has been replaced by a technology that brings with it new dangers, including the ability to censor thought and to place every American under surveillance. Pornography, because of its easy availability on the Internet, has become almost a way of life for many Americans. Illegal and legal drugs continue to claim millions of lives. Addictions have gained such a hold on Americans that they face, as Kennan put it, "a long period of virtual self-enslavement."

He had been right, he told his diary (May 22, 1980), to warn "against the reckless importation into our society . . . and particularly into our great cities, of masses of people of wholly different cultural habits, traditions, and outlooks, incompatible with our own." The demand that those who are in the United States illegally be treated in the same way and receive the same or greater benefits as those who are in the country legally derives from the egalitarianism that Kennan rejected. That also explains the seeming indifference of many Americans to the open borders policy adopted by the Biden administration. That policy has brought in hundreds of thousands of unvetted peoples from countries around the world.

"It seems to me," Kennan wrote to John Lukacs in 1975,

> that we are seeing the pattern of the future throughout the West: a grey, egalitarian uniformity going under the name of moderate socialism—the product of an outlook in which jealousy—jealousy of excellence no less than jealousy of a higher standard of living—is the dominant motif, and in which people are content to accept a colorless shabbiness and dreariness of life, comforted by the reflection that no one lives better or more attractively than themselves, rather than to live better, with the knowledge that someone else lives better still.

If Americans are not to reach the point of no return, they will have to reverse course—with George Kennan acting as their guide. Historical pessimist that he was, he never lost his confidence in teaching, concerning which "one should never inquire too anxiously about the results, for one never knows, or could know, where the seed will fall and take root, nor are the origins of the plant that springs from it always identifiable. Teaching, as I see it is an act of faith."

Kennan wrote those words on February 23, 1984. Years earlier, in his reply to the sixties radicals, he made the same point in fuller detail. "What have you done," a radical student might ask, "to make your views reality?" His reply summed up his entire approach to the mission to which he had dedicated his life: "Being a writer and a teacher, I have felt that the best I could do would be to try to explain, in the proper way and at the proper time, the reasons why I hold these views."

Notes

Chapter 1. A Brief Biography

6. *"The family as I knew it"* John Lukacs, ed., *Through the History of the Cold War: The Correspondence of George F. Kennan and John Lukacs* (Philadelphia: University of Pennsylvania Press, 2010), 91.

7. *"It is after all a habit"* George F. Kennan, "Causes of the Russian Revolution," *Listener* 78 (2014): 559.

7. *"if one could only overthrow"* George F. Kennan, *Encounters with Kennan* (London: Frank Cass, 1979), 71.

8. *"You have a son"* Quoted in John Lewis Gaddis, *George F. Kennan: An American Life* (New York: Penguin, 2011), 12.

8. *"Both of us devoted large portions"* George F. Kennan, *Memoirs, 1925–1950* (Boston: Little, Brown, 1967), 8.

9. *"unbearably lonely, desperately unhappy"* Quoted in Lee Congdon, *George Kennan: A Writing Life* (Wilmington, DE: ISI, 2008), 4.

9. *"The impression of his approach"* Kennan, *Memoirs, 1925–1950*, 14.

9. *"For the first time I felt"* George F. Kennan, *Sketches from a Life* (New York: Pantheon, 1989), 121.

11. *"the state had established its case"* Joseph E. Davies, *Mission to Moscow* (New York: Pocket, 1943), 38.

12. *"because they were sincere fanatical old Bolsheviks"* Quoted in Congdon, *George Kennan*, 13–14.

13. *"a man of incredible criminality"* George F. Kennan, *Russia and the West under Lenin and Stalin* (New York: Mentor, 1960), 241.

15. *"my official loneliness came in fact to an end"* Kennan, *Memoirs, 1925–1950*, 295.

18. *"we are so cut off"* George F. Kennan, letter to President Truman, August 11, 1952, George F. Kennan Papers, Princeton University Library, Princeton, NJ.

18. "*I was interned here in Germany*" George F. Kennan, *Memoirs, 1950–1963* (Boston: Little, Brown, 1972), 159.

18. "*solitude, depth of thought*" Quoted in Gaddis, *George F. Kennan*, 491.

19. "*he never lost the love of life*" George F. Kennan, lecture given at Princeton University, February 26, 1964, George F. Kennan Papers, Princeton University Library, Princeton, NJ.

19. "*close to a world*" Kennan, *Memoirs, 1950–1963*, 130.

20. "*he might have observed*" Kennan, *Memoirs, 1925–1950*, 230.

20. "*the intimate undercurrent of men's lives*" George F. Kennan, "History as Literature," *Encounter*, April 1959, 14.

20. "*Like the actor on the stage*" Kennan, *Memoirs, 1925–1950*, 21.

21. "*I am an eighteenth-century person*" Kennan, *Encounters with Kennan*, 4.

21. "*if you look at the eighteenth century of Europe*" Quoted in Nicholas Lemann, "The Provocateur," *New Yorker*, November 13, 2000, 98.

21. "*the decline of Rome*" Edward Gibbon, "General Observations on the Fall of the Roman Empire in the West," [1776–89.] http://www.ccel.org/g/gibbon/decline/volume1/chap39.htm, accessed October 15, 2021.

21. "*saw Americans as essentially no different*" George F. Kennan, *At a Century's Ending: Reflections, 1982–1995* (New York: W. W. Norton, 1996), 209.

22. "*the United States is somehow exempt*" Richard M. Weaver, *The Southern Essays of Richard M. Weaver*, ed. George M. Curtis III and James J. Thompson Jr. (Indianapolis: Liberty, 1987), 230.

22. "*the problem of sin*" Reinhold Niebuhr, *The Nature and Destiny of Man: A Christian Interpretation*, vol. 1 (New York: Charles Scribner's Sons, 1949), 145.

23. "*The ironic elements in American history*" Reinhold Niebuhr, *The Irony of American History* (New York: Charles Scribner's Sons, 1952), 133.

23. "*feel a grave* Unbehagen" Kennan, *Encounters with Kennan*, 67.

24. "*He was reared a Presbyterian*" Quoted in Gaddis, *George F. Kennan*, 440.

26. "*understanding of and sympathy for our situation*" George F. Kennan, *Around the Cragged Hill: A Personal and Political Philosophy* (New York: W. W. Norton, 1993), 46.

Chapter 2. For a Mature Foreign Policy

27. "*no abstract interest in history*" George F. Kennan, *American Diplomacy, 1900–1950* (New York: Mentor, 1951), 9.

27. "*I have been through one war*" Quoted in Patrick J. Buchanan, *A Republic, Not an Empire: Reclaiming America's Destiny* (Washington, DC: Regnery, 1999), 154.

30. "*not at present prepared*" Quoted in Kennan, *American Diplomacy*, 35.

31. *"by what right we Americans"* Kennan, *American Diplomacy*, 19.

31. *"struck by the contrast"* Kennan, *Memoirs, 1950–1963*, 71.

34. *"started from the premise"* Henry Kissinger, *Diplomacy* (New York: Simon & Schuster, 1994), 39.

34. *"A genuinely national policy"* Herbert Croly, *The Promise of American Life* (New York: The MacMillan Company: 1909 [1912], gutenberg.org/files/14422/14422-h/14422-h.htm#CHAPTER_X.

35. *"no more dangerous delusion"* Kennan, *American Diplomacy*, 88.

36. *"should have the modesty to admit"* Kennan, *American Diplomacy*, 88.

37. *"no one in my position can contribute"* George F. Kennan, *The Kennan Diaries*, ed. Frank Costigliola (New York: W. W. Norton, 2014), 270.

39. *"the characteristic American concept"* George F. Kennan, *Soviet-American Relations, 1917–1920*, vol. 1, *Russia Leaves the War* (Princeton, NJ: Princeton University Press, 1956), 82.

42. *"a man of the eighteenth century"* George F. Kennan, *The Decline of Bismarck's European Order: Franco-Russian Relations, 1875–1890* (Princeton, NJ: Princeton University Press, 1979), 99.

43. *"reconcile personal sympathies and antipathies"* Quoted in Kissinger, *Diplomacy*, 125.

43. *"his long and faithful adherence"* Kennan, *Decline of Bismarck's European Order*, 373.

43. *"intellectually, and in mastery of the subject matter"* Kennan, *Decline of Bismarck's European Order*, 68.

44. *"can be reinforced"* Kennan, *Decline of Bismarck's European Order*, 424.

45. *"master and teacher"* Kennan in Lukacs, *Through the History of the Cold War*, 112.

45. *"was a purely military document"* George F. Kennan, *The Fateful Alliance: France, Russia, and the Coming of the First World War* (New York: Pantheon, 1984), 235.

45. *"in this primitive spirit"* Kennan, *The Fateful Alliance*, 166.

46. *"a democracy can only with great difficulty"* Quoted in Kennan, *Russia and the West*, 130.

47. *"Many varieties of folly and injustice"* Kennan, *At a Century's Ending*, 273–74.

49. *"really to be without obligation"* Kennan, *Around the Cragged Hill*, 70.

50. *"The mere fact that we had stated"* Kennan, *Around the Cragged Hill*, 72.

50. *"Government is an agent"* Kennan, *At a Century's Ending*, 270.

50. *"thinkers as far apart in time"* Kennan, *At a Century's Ending*, 212.

50. *"I do indeed believe in morals"* Kennan in Lukacs, *Through the History of the Cold War*, 18.

51. *"We Americans must realize"* Kennan, *Diaries*, 211.
51. *"We are not under any obligation"* George Kennan, letter to Louis Halle, January 3, 1956, George F. Kennan Papers, Princeton University Library, Princeton, NJ.
52. *"without feeling the obligation"* Kennan, *American Diplomacy*, 49.
52. *"They will soon seep into any legalistic structure"* Kennan, *Diaries*, 171.
52. *"Government always implies and involves power"* Kennan, *Around the Cragged Hill*, 55.

Chapter 3. Russia and Eastern Europe

54. *"I have never had anything but contempt"* Kennan in Lukacs, *Through the History of the Cold War*, 95–96.
54. *"an inordinate touchiness"* Kennan, *Russia and the West*, 235.
57. *"a measure of imagination"* George F. Kennan, *The Nuclear Delusion: Soviet-American Relations in the Atomic Age* (New York: Pantheon, 1976), 42.
58. *"For the eight years I was president"* Quoted in Paul Lettow, *Ronald Reagan and His Quest to Abolish Nuclear Weapons* (New York: Random House, 2005), 6.
59. *"Perhaps having come so close to death"* Quoted in Lettow, *Ronald Reagan and His Quest*, 50.
59. *"Hundreds of millions of people"* Kennan, *At a Century's Ending*, 228.
60. *"a heavily burdened one."* Kennan, *At a Century's Ending*, 327.
61. *"would be the most fateful error of American policy"* George F. Kennan, "NATO Expansion Would Be a Fateful Blunder," *New York Times*, February 6, 1997.
62. *"In the insistence on doing this senseless thing"* Kennan, *Diaries*, 656.
64. *"unable to share that enthusiasm"* Quoted in David Mayers, *George Kennan and the Dilemmas of US Foreign Policy* (New York: Oxford University Press, 1988), 68.
64. *"irresponsible Czechs"* George F. Kennan, *From Prague after Munich: Diplomatic Papers 1938–1940* (Princeton, NJ: Princeton University Press, 1968), 239–40.
65. *"to foster a heretical drifting-away process"* Quoted in Gaddis, *George F. Kennan*, 355.
65. *"the genuine naivety of FDR"* Kennan, *Diaries*, 643.
66. *"the greatest mistake I ever made."* Wilson D. Miscamble, *George F. Kennan and the Making of American Foreign Policy, 1947–1950* (Princeton, NJ: Princeton University Press, 1993), 109.
66. *"They inculcate in their authors"* George F. Kennan, "Spy and Counterspy," *New York Times*, May 18, 1997.

69. *"there is nothing I know"* Kennan, *Diaries*, 360–61.

69. *"Had the Nagy régime not moved"* Kennan, *Encounters with Kennan*, 210.

70. *"A new factor"* Quoted in Gaddis, *George F. Kennan*, 322.

74. *"it was a colossal mistake"* Kennan, *Diaries*, 454.

75. *"the 1956 revolution"* Kennan, *Encounters with Kennan*, 54.

76. *"to see whether"* Kennan, *Diaries*, 567.

78. *"It is not hard to detect"* Kennan, *At a Century's Ending*, 261.

78. *"an enormous and dazzling explosion"* Quoted in Kennan, *At a Century's Ending*, 264.

79. *"I can fairly say"* Kennan, *Diaries*, 602–3.

79. *"a certain naïveté about politics"* Kennan, *At a Century's Ending*, 253.

Chapter 4. The Far and Near East

80. *"no personal familiarity"* Kennan, *American Diplomacy*, 37–38.

81. *"no document on record"* Quoted in Paul J. Heer, *Mr. X and the Pacific: George F. Kennan and American Policy in East Asia* (Ithaca, NY: Cornell University Press, 2018), 12–13.

83. *"There is no requirement"* Quoted in Heer, *Mr. X and the Pacific*, 43.

85. *"Here SCAP had proceeded"* Kennan, *Memoirs, 1925–1950*, 388.

86. *"There is no thornier or more thankless task"* Quoted in Gaddis, *George F. Kennan*, 168.

86. *"Of all the failures"* Kennan, *Diaries*, 211.

86. *"I consider my part"* Kennan, *Memoirs, 1925–1950*, 393.

88. *"it was not tolerable to us"* Quoted in Heer, *Mr. X and the Pacific*, 164.

89. *"Almost everything depends from here on out"* Quoted in Heer, *Mr. X and the Pacific*, 175–76.

90. *"wholly secret, informal and exploratory contacts"* Kennan, *Memoirs, 1950–1963*, 38.

91. *"we must offer the Vietnamese a revolution"* Quoted in Kissinger, *Diplomacy*, 648.

92. *"News of the retaliatory raid in Vietnam"* Kennan, *Diaries*, 431.

92. *"I think it should be our government's aim"* US Senate, Committee on Foreign Relations, *The Vietnam Hearings* (New York: Vintage, 1966), 109.

93. *"I think that without knowing it"* US Senate, *The Vietnam Hearings*, 115.

93. *"one should be very, very careful"* US Senate, *The Vietnam Hearings*, 134.

93. *"if the non-Communist South Vietnamese . . . were incapable"* Quoted in Heer, *Mr. X and the Pacific*, 208.

94. *"Less than at any time in the past"* George F. Kennan, "Introducing Eugene McCarthy," *New York Review of Books* 10, no. 7 (1968).

94. *"One of the principal lessons of the Korean War"* Kissinger, *Diplomacy,* 659.

95. *"a population unhygienic in its habits"* Kennan, *Memoirs, 1925–1950,* 184.

96. *"It has been perfectly clear from the beginning"* Quoted in Congdon, *George Kennan,* 54. Originally in Kennan's letter to "Tom," April 12, 1956. In Kennan Papers, box 31, folder 2.

97. *"I have seen no evidence"* Quoted in Congdon, *George Kennan,* 120.

97. *"Israel's fight against terrorism is our fight"* Quoted in John J. Mearsheimer and Stephen M. Walt, *The Israel Lobby and U.S. Foreign Policy* (New York: Farrar, Straus and Giroux, 2007), 248.

99. *"The dispatch of American armed forces"* Kennan, *Diaries,* 631.

Chapter 5. Lessons Not Learned

101. *"Power must be in the service of some higher value"* Charles Krauthammer, "The Poverty of Realism," *The New Republic,* February 17, 1986.

101. *"Once the United States is committed to spreading its values"* Stephen M. Walt, *The Hell of Good Intentions: America's Foreign Policy Elite and the Decline of U.S. Primacy* (New York: Farrar, Straus and Giroux, 2018), 259.

102. *"interventions on moral principle"* Kennan, *At a Century's Ending,* 273.

104. *"any regime that chooses to call itself Marxist"* Kennan, *Encounters With Kennan,* 57.

104. *Russophobia dates back to the 1054 split* Guy Mettan, *Creating Russophobia: From the Great Religious Schism to Anti-Putin Hysteria* (Atlanta, GA: Clarity Press, 2017).

108. *"Regarding the war in Afghanistan"* Kennan, *Diaries,* 677.

109. *"I would submit that there is more respect to be won"* Kennan, *The Vietnam Hearings,*113.

110. *"I said what everyone in Washington knew"* Quoted in Walt, *The Hell of Good Intentions,* 297n25.

111. *"emphasized that the central purpose of US foreign policy"* Walt, *The Hell of Good Intentions,* 9.

113. *"why we cannot regard Iran"* Kennan, *Diaries,* 662.

114. *"the threat from Iran"* Quoted in Mearsheimer and Walt, *The Israel Lobby,* 295.

114. *"martyrdom-obsessed, non-Western culture"* Quoted in Walt, *The Hell of Good Intentions,* 153.

116. *"I would like to see this country learn to mind its own business"* Kennan in Lukacs, *Through the History of the Cold War,* 15.

116. *"unwillingness to occupy themselves"* Kennan, *Russia and the West,* 360.

117. *"it was reserved for Augustus"* Edward Gibbon, *The History of the Decline and Fall of the Roman Empire,* ed. David Womersley (London: Penguin Books, 1994), 31.

118. *"We have cherished the policy of non-interference"* Quoted in Buchanan, *A Republic, Not an Empire, 152.*

Chapter 6. For a Revivified Society

120. *"It seemed like a relic"* Kennan, *Diaries,* 490.

121. *"entirely similar as regards the inward power"* Oswald Spengler, *The Decline of the West,* vol. 1, trans. Charles Francis Atkinson (New York: Alfred A. Knopf, 1926), 27.

121. *"the Chinese, more prudent and less spoiled"* Kennan, *Diaries,* 500.

122. *"about as controversial as any"* Kennan, *Around the Cragged Hill,* 116–17.

122. *"did not like the term democratic"* Kennan in Lukacs, *Through the History of the Cold War,* 241.

122. *"There can be no question about it"* George F. Kennan, *An American Family: The Kennans: The First Three Generations* (New York: W. W. Norton, 2000), 133.

122. *"for equality their passion is ardent"* Alexis de Tocqueville, *Democracy in America,* vol. 2, trans. Phillips Bradley (New York: Vintage Books, 1945), 102–3.

123. *"when inequality of conditions is the common law of a society"* Tocqueville, *Democracy in America,* vol. 2, 147.

124. *"the bonds of history and memory"* Patrick J. Buchanan, *State of Emergency: The Third World Invasion and Conquest of America* (New York: Macmillan, 2006), 143.

125. *"Equalitarian principles"* Quoted in Gaddis, *George F. Kennan,* 161.

126. *"he viewed with fear and distrust"* George F. Kennan, *The Marquis de Custine and His Russia in 1839* (Princeton, NJ: Princeton University Press, 1971), 72.

126. *"his abhorrence of egalitarianism remained firm"* Kennan, *The Marquis de Custine,* 73.

126. *"There are certain epochs"* Tocqueville, *Democracy in America,* vol. 2, 102.

127. *"has deeply influenced the thinking of millions of people"* Kennan, *Around the Cragged Hill,* 119.

128. *"we find the same familiar vices"* John Kekes, *The Illusions of Egalitarianism* (Ithaca, NY: Cornell University Press, 2003), 6.

130. *"By my own observation"* Kennan, *Around the Cragged Hill,* 121.

131. *"whether it did not actually add something of color and variety"* Kennan, *Sketches From a Life,* 239.

131. *"I simply shudder to think"* Quoted in Congdon, *George Kennan,* 144.

132. *"I am anything but an egalitarian"* Interviews with George F. Kennan, ed. T. Christopher Jespersen (Jackson: University Press of Mississippi, 2002), 153–54.

132. *"Every central power courts and encourages the principle of equality"* Tocqueville, *Democracy in America*, vol. 2, 312.

134. *"like the weakness of the Romans"* Kennan, *Around the Cragged Hill*, 154.

135. *"Our cities will not be flooded"* "Ted Kennedy on Immigration," ontheissues.org/ Celeb/Ted_Kennedy_Immigration.htm.

135. *"Today I see the identity of these people"* Kennan in Lukacs, *Through the History of the Cold War*, 91.

136. *"because they are harder, tougher"* Kennan in Lukacs, *Through the History of the Cold War*, 110.

136. *"the legalization provisions in this act"* reaganlibrary.gov/archives/speech/statement-signing-immigration-reform-and-control-act-1986.

138. *"we are witnessing a progressive demolition of language"* Quoted in Jean-Claude Larchet, *The New Media Epidemic: The Undermining of Society, Family, and Our Own Soul* (Jordanville, NY: Holy Trinity Publications, 2019), 114.

139. *"Seeing this endless prodding and spending"* Jacques Barzun, *From Dawn to Decadence: 500 Years of Western Cultural Life, 1500 to the Present* (New York: HarperCollins, 2000), 778.

Chapter 7. Nature and Faith

144. *"We stand by to witness the rapid decline of family farming"* Kennan, *Around the Cragged Hill*, 102.

144. *"it was a preindustrial life"* Kennan, *Memoirs, 1950–1963*, 128.

145. *"The countryside figures centrally"* Serge Schmemann, *Echoes of a Nativeland: Two Centuries of a Russian Village* (New York: Vintage Books, 2011), 24.

145. *"I can't see the answer"* Kennan, *Encounters With Kennan*, 4.

146. *"Today they sit, passive, bored, and inactive"* Kennan, *Around the Cragged Hill*, 163.

146. *"when he saw some factory in the distance or up close"* Anton Chekhov, *Selected Stories of Anton Chekhov*, trans. Richard Pevear and Larissa Volokhonsky (New York: Modern Library, 2000), 321–22.

147. *"As a physician"* Chekhov, *Selected Stories*, 326.

147. *"arrived at the conclusion that all of this"* Kennan, *Encounters With Kennan*, 205–6.

147. *"For cities there is something sinister and pitiless"* Kennan, *Sketches From a Life*, 130–31.

148. *"abandoned to such of the Third World elements"* Kennan, *Around the Cragged Hill*, 102.

148. *"In place of a world, there is a city"* Spengler, *The Decline of the West*, vol. 1, 32.

148. *There are currently twenty-seven major tent cities* CAUF Society, caufsociety.com/list-of-tent-cities-in-america.

149. *"We don't want to live with police anymore"* Aleksandr Solzhenitsyn, *March 1917: The Red Wheel / Node III (8 March-31 March)*, vol. 1, trans. Marian Schwartz (Notre Dame, IN: University of Notre Dame Press, 2017), 485, 571.

151. *"can one sit by"* Kennan, *Diaries*, 358.

152. *"We will have no pre-arranged sporting activities"* Kennan, *Encounters With Kennan*, 48–49.

152. *"to storm the bastions of society"* George F. Kennan, *Democracy and the Student Left* (New York: Bantam Books, 1968), 8.

153. *"if you're going to change a civilization"* Quoted in Lemann, "The Provocateur," 98.

153. *"the decisive seat of evil"* Kennan, *Democracy and the Student Left*, 8–9.

153. *"The effect of liberty to individuals"* Edmund Burke, *Reflections on the Revolution in France*, ed. Conor Cruise O'Brien (New York: Penguin Books, 1968), 91.

154. *"Every fiber of my being"* Quoted in Kennan, *Democracy and the Student Left*, 65, 39, 43.

154. *"it will take nothing less"* Quoted in Kennan, *Democracy and the Student Left*, 49, 53, 78, 66.

156. *"It was not yet a political movement"* Quoted in Leonard Schapiro, *Turgenev: His Life and Times* (Cambridge: Harvard University Press, 1982), 259.

157. *"frustrated in their efforts"* Kennan, *Democracy and the Student Left*, 192.

158. *"I feel quite crushed in spirit"* Kennan in Lukacs, *Through the History of the Cold War*, 51.

160. *"the breathless and backgroundless preoccupation"* Kennan, *Democracy and the Student Left*, 130.

161. *"McCarthy had no police forces"* Kennan, *Memoirs, 1950–1963*, 220.

161. *"Wherever the authority of the past"* George F. Kennan, *Realities of American Foreign Policy* (New York: W. W. Norton, 1966), 34.

162. *"lost a sense of the fitness of things"* Kennan, *Encounters With Kennan*, 20.

162. *"getting married underground in a subway station"* Barzun, *From Dawn to Decadence*, 782.

162. *"Poor old West"* George F. Kennan, *Decline of the West? George Kennan and His Critics* (Washington, DC: Ethics and Public Policy Center, 1978), 8–9.

163. *"The sexual act itself"* Barzun, *From Dawn to Decadence*, 789.

163. at work as well as at home Larchet, *The New Media Epidemic*, 57.

163. *"a kindly despotism"* Ross Douthat, *The Decadent Society: How We Became the Victims of Our Own Success* (NY: Avid Reader Press, 2020), 137.

164. *"beyond these, there are also troublesome societal conditions"* Kennan, *Around the Cragged Hill*, 158.

164. *"spirit of egalitarianism and materialism"* From a January 1959 draft article that Kennan intended for the *Sunday Times*, Folder 1-E 17, George F. Kennan Papers, Princeton University Library, Princeton, NJ.

165. *"by prohibiting Congress from establishing any particular religion"* Walter A. McDougall, *The Tragedy of U.S. Foreign Policy: How America's Civil Religion Betrayed the National Interest* (New Haven, CT: Yale University Press, 2019), 29.

165. *"utterly secular"* Richard M. Gamble, *In Search of the City on a Hill: The Making and Unmaking of an American Myth* (New York: Continuum, 2012), 154.

165. *"Patriot stands with Patriarch"* Gamble, *In Search of the City on a Hill,* 178.

166. *"to walk in God's ways"* George F. Kennan, "The Relation of Religion to Government," *The Princeton Seminary Bulletin* 62, no. 1 (1969): 45.

166. *"whether there is any such thing as morality"* Kennan, *At a Century's Ending,* 281.

Chapter 8. For a Representative Government

167. *"These regimes differed in certain essential respects"* Kennan, *Around the Cragged Hill,* 61–62.

168. *"the authoritarian regime"* George F. Kennan, "Foreign Policy and Christian Conscience," *Atlantic Monthly,* May 1959.

170. *"I am convinced"* Quoted in Mayers, *George Kennan and the Dilemmas of US Foreign Policy,* 343n.

170. *"towards a pagan Caesarism"* Quoted in Hugh Kay, *Salazar and Modern Portugal* (London: Eyre and Spottiswoode, 1970), 67–69.

170. *"For years Gibbon's dictum"* Kennan, *Democracy and the Student Left,* 180.

171. *"a deep religious faith"* George F. Kennan, "Noble Man," *New York Review of Books* 20, no. 4 (1973).

172. *"has remained for me"* Kennan, *Memoirs, 1925–1950,* 122.

172. *"to concede to these people any serious merit"* Kennan, "Noble Man."

173. *"I am a firm believer"* Kennan, *Diaries,* 569.

174. *"God forbid"* Kennan, *Through the History of the Cold War,* 195.

174. *"I left France scared by the abuses of a false liberty"* Quoted in Kennan, *The Marquis de Custine,* 92.

175. *"It seems to me that there is a pronounced tendency"* George F. Kennan Papers, Princeton University Library, Princeton, NJ.

176. *"Stolypin had grace and style"* George F. Kennan Papers, Princeton University Library, Princeton, NJ.

176. *"It is a reasonable view"* Kennan, *The Marquis de Custine,* 130–31.

177. *"If I thought that this"* Kennan, *Through the History of the Cold War,* 242.

177. *"Many years ago I fell to thinking"* Kennan, *Encounters With Kennan,* 28.

177. *"the vulgar demeanor"* Tocqueville, *Democracy in American,* vol. 1, 211–12.

179. *"Do you think democracy the best government"* Henry Adams, *Democracy: An American Novel* (Columbia, SC: Athena Library, 2020), 24.

181. "in the broad spectrum of political institutions" Kennan, *Diaries*, 463.

182. *"When a nation begins to modify the elective qualification"* Tocqueville, *Democracy in America*, vol. 1, 59.

184. *"If the commentator's words sow despair"* Kennan, *Around the Cragged Hill*, 258–59.

Conclusion: Why Kennan Still Matters

188. *"treat them on the diplomatic level"* Kennan, *Diaries*, 653–54.

189. *"the years 2000. to 2050"* Kennan, *Diaries*, 500.

190. *"a long period of virtual self-enslavement"* Kennan in Lukacs, *Through the History of the Cold War*, 240–41.

190. *"against the reckless importation into our society"* Kennan, *Diaries*, 526.

190. *"It seems to me"* Kennan, *Through the History of the Cold War*, 61–62.

191. *"one should never inquire"* Kennan in Lukacs, *Through the History of the Cold War*, 91.

191. *"Being a writer and a teacher"* Kennan, *Democracy and the Student Left*, 206.

Suggested Readings

George F. Kennan

American Diplomacy, 1900–1950. New York: Mentor Books, 1951.

Around the Cragged Hill: A Personal and Political Philosophy. New York: W. W. Norton, 1993.

At a Century's Ending: Reflections, 1982–1995. New York: W. W. Norton, 1996.

The Cloud of Danger: Current Realities of American Foreign Policy. Boston: Little, Brown, 1977.

The Decline of Bismarck's European Order: Franco-Russian Relations, 1875–1890. Princeton, NJ: Princeton University Press, 1979.

Democracy and the Student Left. New York: Bantam Books, 1968.

The Fateful Alliance: France, Russia, and the Coming of the First World War. New York: Pantheon Books, 1984.

The Kennan Diaries. Edited by Frank Costigliola. New York: W. W. Norton, 2014.

The Marquis de Custine and His Russia in 1839. Princeton, NJ: Princeton University Press, 1971.

Memoirs, 1925–1950. Boston: Little, Brown, 1967.

Memoirs, 1950–1963. Boston: Little, Brown, 1972.

Realities of American Foreign Policy. New York: W. W. Norton, 1966.

Russia, the Atom, and the West: The BBC Reith Lectures, 1957. Oxford: Oxford University Press, 1958.

Russia and the West Under Lenin and Stalin. New York: Mentor, 1961.

Sketches From a Life. New York: Pantheon Books, 1989.

Soviet-American Relations, 1917–1920. Vol. 1. *Russia Leaves the War*. Princeton, NJ: Princeton University Press, 1956.

Soviet-American Relations, 1917–1920. Vol. 2. *The Decision to Intervene*. Princeton, NJ: Princeton University Press. 1958.

Through the History of the Cold War: The Correspondence of George F. Kennan and John Lukacs. Edited by John Lukacs. Philadelphia: University of Pennsylvania Press, 2010.

Other Works

Adams, Henry. *Democracy: An American Novel.* Columbia, SC: Athena Library, 2020.

Barzun, Jacques. *From Dawn to Decadence: 500 Years of Western Cultural Life, 1500 to the Present.* New York: HarperCollins, 2000.

Burke, Edmund. *Reflections on the Revolution in France.* Edited by Conor Cruise O'Brien. New York: Penguin Books, 1968.

Cohen, Stephen F. *War With Russia? From Putin and Ukraine to Trump and Russiagate.* New York: Hot Books, 2019.

Congdon, Lee. *George Kennan: A Writing Life.* Wilmington, DE: ISI Books, 2008.

Gaddis, John Lewis. *George F. Kennan: An American Life.* New York: Penguin Books, 2011.

Gamble, Richard M. *In Search of the City on a Hill: The Making and Unmaking of an American Myth.* New York: Continuum, 2012.

Gibbon, Edward. *The History of the Decline and Fall of the Roman Empire.* Edited by David Womersley. London: Penguin Books, 1995.

Heer, Paul J. *Mr. X and the Pacific: George F. Kennan and American Policy in East Asia.* Ithaca, NY: Cornell University Press, 2018.

Hoebeke, C. H. *The Road to Mass Democracy: Original Intent and the Seventeenth Amendment.* New Brunswick, NJ: Transaction Publishers, 2014.

Kekes, John. *The Illusions of Egalitarianism.* Ithaca, NY: Cornell University Press, 2003.

Kissinger, Henry. *Diplomacy.* New York: Simon & Schuster, 1994.

Kurth, James. *The American Way of Empire: How America Won a World—But Lost Her Way.* Washington, DC: Washington Books, 2019.

Larchet, Jean-Claude. *The New Media Epidemic: The Undermining of Society, Family, and Our Own Soul.* Translated by Archibald Andrew Torrance. Jordanville, NY: Holy Trinity Publications, 2019.

Lukacs, John. *George Kennan: A Study in Character.* New Haven, CT: Yale University Press, 2007.

McDougall, Walter A. *The Tragedy of U.S. Foreign Policy: How America's Civil Religion Betrayed the National Interest.* New Haven, CT: Yale University Press, 2019.

Mearsheimer, John J. *The Great Delusion: Liberal Dreams and International Realities.* New Haven, CT: Yale University Press, 2018.

Mearsheimer, John J., and Stephen M. Walt. *The Israel Lobby and U.S. Foreign Policy.* New York: Farrar, Straus and Giroux, 2007.

Tocqueville, Alexis de. *Democracy in America.* Vols. 1 and 2. New York: Vintage Books, 1945.

Travis, Frederick F. *George Kennan and the American-Russian Relationship, 1865–1924.* Athens: Ohio University Press, 1990.

US Senate, Committee on Foreign Relations. *The Vietnam Hearings.* New York: Vintage, 1966.

Walt, Stephen M. *The Hell of Good Intentions: America's Foreign Policy Elite and the Decline of U.S. Primacy.* New York: Farrar, Straus and Giroux, 2018.

Warnecke, Grace Kennan. *Daughter of the Cold War.* Pittsburgh, PA: University of Pittsburgh Press, 2018.

Index